Russian History

A Captivating Guide to the History of Russia, Including Events Such as the Mongol Invasion, the Napoleonic Invasion, Reforms of Peter the Great, the Fall of the Soviet Union, and More

Free Bonus from Captivating History
(Available for a Limited time)

Hi History Lovers!

Now you have a chance to join our exclusive history list so you can get your first history ebook for free as well as discounts and a potential to get more history books for free! Simply visit the link below to join.

Captivatinghistory.com/ebook

Also, make sure to follow us on:

Twitter: @Captivhistory

Facebook: Captivating History:@captivatinghistory

Contents

Introduction

Russia, or the Russian Federation as it is officially known, is the world's largest country and covers almost a sixth of the global landmass. The country is often associated with harsh climates and autocratic government. The shadow of communism and the Cold War continues to influence global attitudes towards Russia. The Russian state – with regard to its territory – only took shape in the early modern era, around the turn of the eighteenth century. It claims descent from a political entity known as Kievan Rus, centered in the capital of modern Ukraine, although the connection is at best indirect. The questions of historical legitimacy have attracted greater interest in the context of recent political and military conflict between Russia and Ukraine. The process of the formation of the Russian state took place over several centuries and at several junctures history could have taken a different course. This book serves as an overview of Russian history over the span of more than a millennium, from the foundation of the Russian state by the Viking prince Rurik in 862 AD until the collapse of the Soviet Union at the end of 1991.

For the purposes of simplicity, the book takes a chronological approach. Part 1 (Chapters 1-6) covers the Russian state, referred to by contemporaries as Rus, from its foundation by Rurik until the extinction of the Rurikid dynasty at the end of the 16th century. This section covers some of the most important processes which shaped Russian history, including the Christianization of Rus by Prince Vladimir the Great, the Mongol conquest, the rise of Moscow and the efforts to achieve independence from Mongol and Tatar overlords. Part 2 (Chapters 7-13) charts the fortunes of Russia under the rule of the Romanov dynasty. During the 300 years of Romanov rule, Russia established itself as a major European power, establishing control of the Baltic under Peter the Great, expanding southwest under Catherine the Great, and defeating Napoleon under Alexander I. This era ended in 1917 in the midst of war and revolution. Part 3 (Chapters 14-18) covers the period of communist rule in Russia. In less than a century the Soviet Union aimed to build a radical socialist utopia, established a sinister dictatorship, contributed to victory in the Second World War, and struggled with the United States for global hegemony before its demise in the 1980s.

This book primarily presents a political history of Russia. Although it is possible to outline a history of Russia using a social, economic, or cultural perspective, history is usually simplest to follow when associated with rulers and individuals. This approach is made easier by the fact that Russian history is full of fascinating personalities, both men and women, from Saint Olga of Kiev and Catherine the Great to Ivan the Terrible and Josef Stalin. Through these individuals, this book seeks to bring Russian history to life for readers. Although some of the episodes mentioned in this book may appear fantastical or incredible, or seeming to be stories from the past with little relevance to modern society, they have shaped the development of the Russian state in its current form. Nation-states around the world look into the pages of history to inform national identity, and Russia is no different. This book strives to identify some of the key themes of Russian history and to highlight their importance both in contemporary Russia and worldwide.

Part 1 – Medieval Rus

Chapter 1 – The Foundation of Rus

Several tribes and peoples occupied what is now Eastern Europe in the centuries following the collapse of the Roman Empire. The major ethnic group were the Slavs, a term derived from *slovo*, meaning "word," denoting people who spoke the same language. By the 6th and 7th centuries, there were three major branches of Slavic tribes. The East Slavs occupied much of the Russian heartland and Ukraine, together with parts of modern-day Belarus. The South Slavs occupied much of the Balkan peninsula, while the West Slavs were based in what is now Poland. Some Slavs lived under the rule of Turkic peoples such as the Avars, Bulgars, and Khazars. Baltic tribes such as the Prus, Livs, Curs, Chuds, lived by the Baltic Sea, while much of the north and east was occupied by Finno-Ugric peoples. Though subsequent conflict and conquest resulted in the migration and displacement of some of these peoples, there is much genealogical evidence for mixed marriages and family relations. Consequently, the ethnic make-up of Russians today, while predominantly Slavic, also includes Finnish, Scandinavian, Turkic and Baltic elements.

Most of these peoples were pagans who worshipped deities based on natural phenomena, even if their gods had different names. The most important god in Eastern Slavic paganism was Perun, the God of Thunder, who may be most closely compared to Thor in Norse mythology, or Zeus in the Greek pantheon. Perun's counterpart and opponent was Volos, most frequently associated with the earth and waters. Slavic pagans also saw spirits inhabiting lakes, rivers, and forests. The invocation of natural phenomena and spirits was a key part of pagan rituals and usually associated with the agricultural calendar. Some of the peasant folk dances which originated in pagan rituals invoking the abundant earth continue to survive to this day in rural communities.

In the 9th century, the Slavic lands began to be subjected to raids from the north by Varangians, eastern Vikings who sought to establish a route to Constantinople, the great capital of the Byzantine Empire. The Varangians appear to have managed to exact tribute from some tribes, though the tribes soon rebelled and refused further payment. These tribes began to fight among themselves and any form of law and order that had previously existed disintegrated. According to the Russian Primary Chronicle, compiled in the early 12th century, the warring tribes were unable to establish a peaceful settlement by themselves and decided to invite a foreign prince to arbitrate over them and restore order. They petitioned a group of Varangians known as the Rus (according to one theory, after their red hair) in the following manner: "Our land is great and rich, but there is no order in it. Come to rule and reign over us."

It is debatable whether the Rus were invited by all the warring tribes to rule over them, or whether they made alliances with various factions which allowed them to incrementally consolidate their control over what is now northwestern Russia. In any case, the foundation of the Russian state is said to have taken place in 862 with the arrival of the Varangian prince Rurik (862-79) and his two younger brothers. After gaining control of Ladoga, Rurik established himself in a settlement called Holmgard, located on the eastern bank of the River Volkhov as it flows into Lake Ilmen, several miles to the south of the later city of Novgorod. His brothers Sineus and Truvor were based in Beloozero and Izborsk respectively. Within a couple of years, the younger brothers died and Rurik became sole ruler of the land now known as the Rus. From his base in Novgorod, Rurik sent groups men to settle and conquer new territories, expanding his authority to the south and east.

Among Rurik's followers were two prominent individuals named Askold and Dir. They were sent to Constantinople, the capital of the great Byzantine Empire, which the Slavs called Tsargrad (Caesar's city). On their way down the River Dniepr, they came across the city of Kiev which at that time was largely populated by a Slavic tribe called the Polianians, but under the rule of the Khazars, a Turkic tribe whose rulers had converted to Judaism. Askold and Dir attacked the Khazars and managed to conquer Kiev, establishing their own power base while Rurik continued to rule in Novgorod. Over time greater numbers of Varangians followed and settled in Kiev and its hinterland, mixing and integrating with the local Slavic population.

When Rurik died in 879 AD, his son Igor was still a young child and unable to take over the reins of power. He therefore left his realm to his kinsman Oleg (879-912), thought to be a brother-in-law. Over the course of the next three years, Oleg led an army of his Slavic and Baltic subjects in order to establish his authority in territories which had rebelled against the Rus upon Rurik's death. When he arrived in Kiev in 882 AD, he saw that Askold and Dir were ruling over a magnificent and prosperous city and enjoying luxuries greater than his own, even though he was their sovereign lord. On this basis he believed that Askold and Dir were potential challengers to his authority and devised a plan to eliminate them. He hid his men in his boats and laid ambush on the Kievan rulers. Disguising himself as a messenger, he beckoned them to the river bank, whereupon the soldiers emerged from their boats. "You are not princes nor even of princely stock, but I am of princely birth," Oleg pronounced to the unsuspecting Askold and Dir. He then presented Igor to them, informing them that the young child was the son of Rurik. At this point the soldiers rushed forward and killed both Askold and Dir.

Through this means Oleg gained control of Kiev. He proclaimed that Kiev would be his capital and the mother of all Russian cities, relegating Novgorod to a subordinate tribute-paying role. For the two following centuries Kiev remained the capital of the Russian cities and its ruler took the title *Velikiy Knyaz*, Grand Prince. The state is now known to history as the Kievan Rus, but this term was not coined until the nineteenth century. Nevertheless, Oleg's decision to move his capital southwards had significant developments for the Russian state. The center of gravity in Russia moved from the Baltic north to the southern steppes. Not only was the land more fertile, but the city of Kiev was strategically located on the River Dniepr, which flows into the Black Sea. Oleg also moved his center of power closer to Constantinople and the Byzantine Empire.

The Byzantine Empire was the Eastern, Greek-speaking half of the Roman Empire and remained an imperial power after the fall of Rome in the west. Although by the 9th century AD it was no longer as extensive as during its zenith under the Emperor Justinian in the 6th century AD, the Christian empire remained one of Europe's most powerful and wealthiest states. The relationship with the Byzantine Empire became a key factor in the foreign policy of the Kievan Rus. The two states were in conflict on several occasions. The Russian Primary Chronicle relates an assault on Constantinople in 866 AD led by Askold and Dir, who headed an armada of two hundred ships. The Byzantine Emperor Michael III was isolated and it seemed that the city would fall to the invaders. With few men capable of protecting the city, the inhabitants turned to divine intercession. The Emperor and the Patriarch of Constantinople prayed all night, sang hymns, and carried the Virgin Mary's robe into the sea. A great storm soon arose, stirring up the waves and causing the Russian boats to run aground. Suffering heavy losses, the Russians turned back to Kiev.

This unsuccessful attempt did not dissuade the Russians from making further efforts to capture Constantinople. In 907 AD Prince Oleg campaigned against the Greeks and negotiated a favorable peace treaty with the Emperor. The treaty stipulated that Russian merchants trading in Constantinople would receive provisions from the Byzantine state, and that they could carry out their business activities without being subject to taxation. Over the years Kiev and Constantinople would form a close trading relationship. In return, certain restrictions were placed upon the Russian merchants so that they would not pose a threat to the city. To seal the treaty, the Greeks swore an oath on the cross while the pagan Russians swore on their weapons and to the gods Perun and Volos. Upon his return to Kiev, Oleg was hailed by his Slavic subjects for his artful diplomacy and proclaimed "Oleg the Wise."

In 912, after further strengthening relations with the Byzantine Empire, Oleg died and was succeeded by Igor (912-45), Rurik's son. Like his predecessor, Igor is said to have ruled over Rus for 33 years, although only the final years of his reign are documented. Near the end of his life he embarked on two campaigns against Constantinople, in 941 and 944 respectively. The Primary Chronicle claims that on this second campaign Igor sailed at the head of ten thousand vessels, but this number is surely unrealistic. Nevertheless, the Russian fleet was formidable and once again the Byzantine Emperor was forced to sue for peace. As part of the terms of this new settlement the Russians were bought off with a large quantity of gold, and their trading privileges in Constantinople were extended. Russians in Constantinople also enjoyed the same judicial rights and punishments as the subjects of the Emperor.

Igor's campaign in Constantinople coincided with a Russian expedition against the Arabs in the Caucasus. This expedition seems to have been commanded by a warlord named Sveinald, who was nominally under Igor's service although the sources do not say whether Igor sanctioned the expedition. Sveinald's raid appears to have been very lucrative as he enjoyed great wealth. Upon Igor's return from Kiev, his retinue observed that Sveinald was living in greater luxury than the princely court and encouraged the prince to take measures to increase his wealth so it would be greater than that of his commander. Motivated by these considerations, in 945 Prince Igor led his men against a Slavic tribe called the Drevlians to demand greater tribute. His requests were duly granted and the seemingly satisfied Kievans duly departed and turned back to their capital.

On the return journey, Igor devised a plan to extract even more tribute from the Drevlians and turned back with a few men, allowing his main army to continue their journey to Kiev. When the Drevlians received news that Igor was on his way back, they consulted with Mal, their ruling prince. Prince Mal decided that they could no longer continue to appease Igor, since every time he would come back to demand more until the Drevlians had no more tribute to give. Taking advantage of the fact that Igor was without his army, they set upon his small retinue and captured him. They took him to their capital at the town of Iskorosten and executed him. According to a Byzantine source, "They had bent down two birch trees to the prince's feet and tied them to his legs; then they let the trees straighten again, thus tearing the prince's body apart." Cruel forms of execution are often attested to in early sources, although most likely this description was inspired by artistic license. The name of the Drevlian tribe derives from the word *derevo* which means tree in the Slavic language.

Chapter 2 – The Christianization of Rus

Upon his death, Igor left behind a young son named Svyatoslav (945-72). The child was around three years old when he succeeded to his father's title of Grand Prince of Kiev. Igor's widow Olga was named regent for her young son, while Sveinald was appointed commander-in-chief. The Drevlians decided to use this opportunity to exploit the weakness of Kiev and to change their subordinate status as tributaries to Kiev. They planned to invite Olga to marry Prince Mal, informing her that he had been a good prince and was wronged by the capricious Igor. By doing so, they hoped to take control of the young Svyatoslav and ensure that he would be friendly to the Drevlians. With this plan in mind, they sent twenty respected men as emissaries to the Kievan court to meet Olga.

Olga received the dignitaries well and told them she was willing to marry their prince. She bade them to return to their boats for the night, telling them that she hoped to receive them officially in the presence of her subjects. She assured them that they would be carried in their boat through the city. The following morning, orders were given for the Drevlians be carried through the streets of Kiev in their boat as they had been promised. They assumed an air of pride and looked on disdainfully at the local population. In their triumph the ambassadors did not suspect that Olga prepared a ditch in front of her palace, into which they were deposited and buried alive. Olga knew that killing twenty men would not be sufficient to defeat her enemies. She therefore sent word to the Drevlians that if they were really serious about her marrying their prince, they must send all their distinguished men to escort her to Drevlian territory. When these men arrived, Olga invited them to the bathhouse and promised to meet them after they had bathed. Once the emissaries were inside, she gave the orders to lock the doors and burn down the wooden bathhouse, thus trapping the men amongst the flames.

Finally, Olga sent a message to the Drevlians that she was on her way, and ordered them to prepare large quantities of mead and honey. She arrived at Igor's tomb and expressed her desire to hold a funeral feast in his honor, inviting all the local dignitaries and ordering her followers to serve them. When the Drevlians were completely drunk, she ordered her men to slaughter them. Five thousand men were killed in the operation, and Olga requested further reinforcements to subdue her enemies completely. She led this force to the gates of Iskorosten and laid siege to the city. After a year of campaigning, she was unable to capture the Drevlian capital. She realized that she could not take the city using traditional military means and devised yet another deception strategy. She signaled that she was prepared to abandon her siege if the Drevlians would pay tribute to Kiev. Offered honey and furs by the Drevlians, Olga informed them that she wished only to extract a small price – three sparrows and pigeons from each household. The Drevlians delivered the birds to Olga and returned to their homes, rejoicing that they were finally at peace. Olga ordered her men to attach small amounts of sulfur wrapped in cloth to the sparrows and pigeons. When they were set free, they returned to the city and duly set fire to their nests. The city was set ablaze and the inhabitants were massacred by Kievan soldiers as they escaped from the city.

Having successfully subdued the Drevlians and extinguished any prospect of further rebellion, Olga returned to Kiev and ruled over a peaceful realm. In 955 she embarked on a journey to Constantinople where she was met by the Emperor Constantine VII. The Emperor was impressed by her beauty and wisdom and wished to make her his empress. Olga replied that she was still pagan and would only agree to be baptized if the Emperor himself were to preside over the ceremony. She was duly baptized by the Patriarch and the Emperor and was happy to have joined the Christian faith. When Constantine proposed marriage, however, Olga answered that since he was her godfather, the proposed marriage was illegal under Christian law and she had no choice but to refuse his suit. The Emperor smiled and praised Olga for her wisdom, recognizing he had been outwitted. The Russian princess sailed back to Kiev with her ship laden with gifts from Constantine.

Upon her return to Kiev, Olga hoped to persuade her son and his subjects to convert to Christianity. Her efforts were in vain. Svyatoslav replied to his mother that conversion Christianity would encourage his warlike race to become meek and humble. Brought up by the great warrior Sveinald, Svyatoslav became a skilled fighter and had military ambitions. By the time he came of age, he was eager to go on campaign. Over the course of eight years between 964 and 972, Svyatoslav conducted a series of campaigns against a wide range of enemies. In 965 he successfully defeated the Khazars in battle and conquered the Khaganate of Khazaria. In 967, allied to the Byzantine Empire, he initiated a war against the First Bulgarian Empire and precipitated its collapse. In 968 he captured the strategic trading center of Pereyaslavets from the Bulgarians.

During Svyatoslav's absence from Kiev, the city was besieged by the Pechenegs, a nomadic Turkic tribe. Olga and Svyatoslav's young sons managed to escape the encirclement to join a small relieving force. Their presence raised a cheer in the camp that the Pechenegs lifted the siege under the impression that Svyatoslav had arrived. Once Kiev was safe, Svyatoslav received a letter from Kiev in which he was chastised by his mother for placing Kiev in danger. He duly returned to defeat the Pechenegs, but the following year he informed his subjects that he would relocate his capital to Pereyaslavets, leaving his eldest son Yaropolk to rule Kiev. The decision was unpopular and Olga begged Svyatoslav to reconsider, but he stuck to his decision. Olga died three days after Svyatoslav's departure to Pereyaslavets and was subsequently honored as the first Russian saint.

Svyatoslav's incredible victories incited jealousy among his Byzantine allies, who reneged on the alliance and attacked the Russians. In 971 they marched against Pereyaslavets with 100,000 men. Inside the city, Svyatoslav had only 10,000 men bearing arms. Nevertheless, the Russian prince commanded his men to fight or die, and the valiant soldiers managed to repel the attack and force the invaders to withdraw. Prince Svyatoslav then assumed the offensive and pursued the defeated enemy to Constantinople. As he approached the imperial capital, he was met by Greek emissaries who presented him with gold and silk. When the warrior prince refused these offerings, the envoys returned with a collection of weapons. Svyatoslav found these gifts more amenable and gave his thanks to the Emperor. Recognizing that Svyatoslav was a formidable warrior, the Byzantines begged him to go no further, but to accept tribute instead. Svyatoslav duly negotiated a favorable treaty with the Emperor and left Constantinople. On his return, he was ambushed by the Pechenegs, who were informed by the Greeks that Svyatoslav was return to Pereyaslavets with a small retinue. The nomads set upon him and killed him, turning his skull into a drinking vessel for their chieftain. Pereyaslavets was taken by the Greeks and the Russian court returned to Kiev.

Upon his death in 972, Svyatoslav left behind two legitimate sons; Yaropolk (972-80) in Kiev and Oleg, who ruled over the Drevlians in the town of Dereva. Svyatoslav's illegitimate son, Vladimir, was based in Novgorod. The two elder brothers fell out with each other and in 977 Yaropolk killed Oleg and seized his lands. Vladimir had sided with Oleg in the fratricidal conflict and decided to flee from Novgorod fearing for his own life. Over the course of the next two years Vladimir gathered supporters from his distant brethren in Norway and in 980 embarked on a campaign against Yaropolk. Leading a large force of supporters and Varangian allies against Kiev, Vladimir forced his half-brother to capitulate. The unfortunate Yaropolk was later assassinated by Varangian mercenaries. Vladimir (980-1015), illegitimate and youngest son of Svyatoslav, thus emerged as Grand Prince of Kiev.

Like his father, Vladimir was a committed pagan and celebrated his victory by erecting idols of pagan gods both in Kiev and throughout his cities. Vladimir's uncle Dobrynya was sent to govern Novgorod, and built a large wooden totem depicting the thunder god Perun towering over the west bank of the Volkhov River. In the initial years of his reign, Vladimir followed his father's example and embarked on a series of successful military campaigns. In around 987, Vladimir is said to have received ambassadors from the Muslim Bulgars who sought to encourage him to adopt their faith. Enquiring about their lifestyle, the Muslims replied that they refrained from pork and wine. Vladimir was unable to accept these restrictions. "Drinking," said he, "is the joy of the Russians. We cannot exist without that pleasure." There followed German emissaries, who encouraged Vladimir to convert to Catholicism. The prince, realizing that he would have to submit to the authority of the Pope, rejected their religion. The Jewish Khazars came next, and described themselves as God's chosen people. Vladimir enquired of them that if this were the case, why they had been banished from their homeland and forced into exile. Finally, a Greek scholar came to Kiev and explained at length the Orthodox religion.

After receiving all the missionaries, Vladimir was inclined to convert to the Greek faith. However, he was hesitant to do so and his advisors cautioned him against accepting the Greeks at their word, since the Russians had suffered many times on the basis of Byzantine deceit. Vladimir therefore resolved to send his own ambassadors to visit the lands of the Muslims, Catholics, Jews, and Orthodox in turn and return with their observations. When they returned to Kiev, they reported to Vladimir and the leading nobles that they saw the Muslims praying in their mosques in silence, burying their heads to the ground. Their faith was solemn and joyless. They entered the Catholic churches, which were richly adorned but devoid of spirituality. "Then we went to Greece, and the Greeks led us to the edifices where they worship their God, and we knew not whether we were in heaven or on earth." Vladimir, who remembered that his grandmother Saint Olga had been an Orthodox Christian herself, thus resolved to convert his people to Orthodox Christianity.

This is the tale of "the baptism of Rus" in 988 AD, as presented in the Primary Chronicle. While this is a popular version and provides an interesting insight into Russian stereotypes of foreign peoples and their religions, the actual circumstances of the conversion appear to have been encouraged by more prosaic factors such as military and strategic implications. At the end of the 10th century, the Russians and Greeks were seeking a closer relationship. Vladimir hoped to forge an alliance with the Byzantine Emperor Basil II by marrying his sister Anna. In order to marry the Greek princess Vladimir agreed to become a Christian and was baptized in the city of Kherson, a Greek city recently conquered from the Byzantine Empire. In the process, Vladimir sought to establish Christianity as his state religion and the Greeks sent Orthodox priests to evangelize the Russian people. As ruler of Rus both in name and in fact, Vladimir achieved what his grandmother attempted and failed. In the meantime, Vladimir ordered the pagan idols to be broken and churches to be built in their place, employing Greek artisans to build and decorate them.

Vladimir fell ill and died in 1015 and was canonized as Saint Vladimir. He had twelve children, some of whom predeceased him. He had hoped to leave his realm to his sons Boris and Gleb, whose mother was the Byzantine princess Anna Porphyrogenita, whom

Vladimir had married after his conversion to Christianity. Both princes were away from Kiev when they heard of their father's death. Meanwhile, political power in Kiev was seized by Svyatopolk (1015-19), Vladimir's son from Yaropolk's wife. Svyatopolk gathered his supporters and sought to seize the entire realm. Boris and Gleb were both murdered by Svyatopolk's men, in the process becoming the first Christian martyrs in Russia. Meanwhile, Yaroslav, son of Vladimir's first wife, heard that his brothers had been slain and vowed to confront Svyatopolk with an army of Novgorodians. A bitter civil war ensued, during which the city of Kiev changed hands three times. Eventually, Yaroslav emerged the victor and Svyatopolk died as he fled to Bohemia.

Chapter 3 – The Fragmentation and Subjugation of Rus

The reign of Yaroslav (1019-54) proved to be a golden age for Kievan Rus. Yaroslav was a learned man and surrounded himself with books, earning him the nickname Yaroslav the Wise. He wrote many texts on Christianity which were distributed among his people, continuing his father's efforts to enlighten his subjects. Grand Prince Yaroslav left behind a lasting material legacy in his cities. He had founded the city of Yaroslavl on the upper Volga while still a minor prince. He defeated the Chuds in the Baltic and founded the city of Yuryev, modern-day Tartu in Estonia. He built St. Sophia's Cathedral in Kiev, inspired by the Hagia Sophia Cathedral in Constantinople. The thirteen-domed cathedral became the royal mausoleum for the Kievan princes and remains one of the most popular tourist attractions in Kiev. He also built a great citadel in the city, of which only the so-called Golden Gate remains. The famous Pechersk Monastery of the Caves, inspired by the Greek monastery at Mount Athos, was also built during Yaroslav's reign.

When Yaroslav died in 1054, he instituted a law of succession for his sons and descendants. He sought to put an end to the fratricidal conflicts of his own and his father's generation. He stipulated that his eldest son would succeed him as Grand Prince of Kiev, while his other sons were sent to rule other key Russian principalities. When the eldest son died, he would not be succeeded by his son, but by his eldest surviving brother, usually the Prince of Novgorod. Only after the extinction of a generation of brothers would the throne pass to the next generation, with the condition that the descendants of minor princes who did not succeed to the Kievan throne were excluded from future succession. Through this system of lateral succession, Yaroslav hoped that brothers would no longer be compelled to fight against each other but would one day succeed to the Kievan throne provided they were still living.

Subsequent developments were to show that Yaroslav's remedy was worse than the illness he sought to cure. At the beginning, Yaroslav's sons Izyaslav (1054-73), Svyatoslav II (1073-77), and Vsevolod (1077-92) heeded their father's words and supported each other. They waged a campaign against their nephew Rostislav, whose father Vladimir had died in 1052, leaving him with no prospect of succession to his uncles' principalities. The princely triumvirate broke up in 1073 when Svyatoslav and Vsevolod turned against their eldest brother and expelled him from Kiev. Thus, Yaroslav's succession laws did nothing to prevent conflicts between brothers, cousins, uncles and nephews who ruled over an increasingly fragmented collection of principalities under Kiev's nominal authority.

Over time these internecine conflicts among Russian princes led to the fragmentation of the Kievan state. While Kiev remained the political and spiritual center of the Russian lands and the title of Grand Prince of Kiev was still the ultimate prize, central authority in Kiev diminished and the Russian principalities had their own princes and political structures independent from the capital. Among the alternative political systems that emerged during this period of fragmentation was that of Novgorod. The city of Novgorod, which ranked second in prestige to Kiev among Russian cities, had enjoyed wide-ranging privileges since the days of Yaroslav. Unlike many other Russian cities, Novgorod had a wealthy and powerful merchant community and was a member of the Hanseatic League. As Kiev's authority weakened, the Novgorodians consolidated and strengthened their privileges both with regard to Kiev and to their own ruling prince. In 1136, the Novgorod Veche – a popular assembly – voted to overthrow Prince Vsevolod Mstislavich. They established the Republic of Novgorod in which the Veche was the supreme governing institution. Although there were still princes who ruled in Novgorod, their authority was dependent on what powers the Veche granted them. During the Novgorod Republic, the Prince of Novgorod was effectively a military leader with limited political authority. In order to emphasize that true sovereignty lay with the city and its people, Novgorodians often referred to their municipality as Lord Novgorod the Great.

Over time, some of these subordinate principalities absorbed their neighbors and increased their territorial scope. By the mid-1100s, the Principality of Vladimir-Suzdal became sufficiently powerful to challenge Kiev itself. The city of Vladimir appears to have been founded in 1108 by Prince Vladimir of Rostov-Suzdal, who would become Grand Prince Vladimir II Monomakh (1113-25). Monomakh's reign in Kiev, during which he passed a number of popular social reforms, was considered a golden age in the city before its eventual decline and fall, ironically at the hands of the city he founded. Incidentally, the Russian Primary Chronicle, one of the key historical sources for medieval Russia, was produced during the reign of Monomakh by Sylvester, Prior of St. Michael's Monastery in Kiev.

Monamakh's grandson Andrey Bogolyubsky (1157-1174) made Vladimir the capital of his principality, which was renamed Vladimir-Suzdal. As a mark of his ambition, he styled himself the Grand Prince of Vladimir-Suzdal. He was responsible for building the grand Cathedral of the Annunciation and the Cathedral of Saint Demetrius nearby in the city's citadel. He also ordered the construction of the Church of the Intercession on the Nerl several miles along the River Klyazma. This small perfectly-proportioned, single-domed church is usually considered to be the most beautiful of all Russian churches. In 1164 he petitioned the Orthodox Patriarch in Constantinople for the establishment of a metropolitan see in Vladimir to rival that of Kiev. The petition was unsuccessful, but in 1169 he led an army against Kiev and sacked the city. He forcibly transferred the metropolitan see in Kiev to his capital in Vladimir. By moving the spiritual center of Russia to Vladimir, Prince Andrey consolidated the city of Vladimir's position as the political center of the Russian state. The title of Grand Prince of Kiev continued to exist separately but it became less prestigious during the ascendency of the city of Vladimir.

Although Andrey Bogolyubsky was unable to maintain control over Kiev, the damage the city suffered in 1169 meant that it never recovered its former position. The new capital of Vladimir would remain the leading city in Rus for two centuries. Andrey's brother Vsevolod III (1177-1212) achieved considerable military successes against the principality of Ryazan, the main rival to Vladimir-Suzdal. During Vsevolod's reign, Vladimir enjoyed great prosperity and ruled over much of northeastern Rus. However, Vsevolod's death in 1212 destabilized the internal political situation. Vsevolod had fourteen children, which earned him the nickname Vsevolod the Big Nest. Yet such a big nest was a recipe for disaster and led to conflict amongst his sons. Vsevolod had disinherited his eldest son Konstantin and left his realm to his third son Yury, who became Yury II (1212-16; 1218-38) upon his father's death. Konstantin and Yury then fought a bitter civil war which ended with Konstantin's capture of Vladimir in 1216.

Although Yury II regained the throne in 1218 upon Konstantin's death that year, his reign was not a happy one. In 1223 the Mongols made their first foray into Russian territory and defeated a Kievan force under its Grand Prince Mstislav III, who was executed in the aftermath of the Battle of the Kalka River. Russia did not yet fall under Mongol subjugation as the invaders soon turned around and returned to Asia, but in 1237 they returned with a vengeance. The invasion force under Batu Khan approached from the southeast and attacked Ryazan. The city's request for aid from Vladimir was not granted, since Yury regarded Ryazan as his principality's major rival. In December the city was captured by the Mongols, who then turned their attention to Vladimir itself, capturing the capital in February 1238. Yury retreated and gathered a new army, but this new force was soundly defeated by the Mongols and the Grand Prince was killed.

Over the next three years the Mongol armies swept across the Russian lands, sacking major cities on the way. A legendary tale tells of the city of Kitezh, which disappeared under the waters of Lake Svetolyar when the Mongol hordes approached. By 1240 the old capital of Kiev was captured. Only Pskov and Novgorod to the northwest avoided destruction by negotiating surrender. Thus, the Russian lands became part of the Mongol empire which stretched from the Pacific almost to the Baltic. With the death of Kublai Khan in 1294, the Mongol empire split into four major entities. The Russian portion was called the Golden Horde. The khans of the Golden Horde ruled Rus from their capital of Sarai located on the lower reaches of the Volga River, near modern-day Astrakhan. The Mongols abandoned their nomadic lifestyles and settled alongside the Tatars, a Turkic tribe which inhabited the southern steppes. Over time intermarriage between the Mongols and Tatars created a single race. Initially, the Golden Horde did not intervene much in 'internal affairs.' The Russian princes were allowed to fight each other just as they had done for more than two centuries. The Golden Horde expressed their authority in two main ways. Firstly, the Russian princes were obliged to pay tribute to the khan. Secondly, the Grand Prince of Vladimir had to travel to Sarai to receive a *yarlyk*, a document which authorized him to rule in the name of the khan.

In many ways, the threat of the Mongols in the east less important than the threats facing Rus from the west. The Novgorod First

Chronicle states that in 1240 a Swedish army invaded Novgorod, seeking to take advantage of the crisis precipitated by the Mongol invasion and take control of Novgorod's trade networks. The twenty-year-old Prince Alexander Yaroslavich, grandson of Vsevolod the Big Nest, led a small army of Novgorodians to confront the Swedes, who had captured the mouth of the River Neva and were marching inland. Despite the numerical disparity, Alexander went on the offensive won an unlikely victory and repelled the unsuspecting invaders. For his efforts he was given the honorific name Nevsky, derived from the River Neva. Aside from Russian sources, the evidence for the Battle of the Neva is limited, and it is more likely that it was a small border skirmish which assumed greater proportions. Nevertheless, this battle made the reputation of Alexander Nevsky, who would be celebrated as one of the greatest warrior princes in Russian history.

At the same time, the Teutonic Order – the crusader state which was based in the Baltic – invaded Pskov from the west. The invasion was part of an effort by the papacy to force Eastern Orthodox Christians to accept papal supremacy in Rome. Prince Alexander was keen to go to help Pskov, but was unable to do so. In 1241, Alexander successfully launched an offensive in order to retake Pskov from the Teutons and raided Crusader territory before retreating east. He was pursued by a force led by Bishop Hermann of Dorpat (Tartu), who pursued him across the frozen Lake Peipus (Lake Chudskoe in Russian). Alexander arranged his forces in a defensive formation with his cavalry on the flanks. The Teutonic knights attacked in a wedge formation, led by their formidable heavy cavalry. As his infantry cushioned the impact in the center, engaging in desperate hand-to-hand fighting, Alexander ordered his cavalry on both flanks to encircle the enemy, inflicting heavy losses on Hermann's army. Although tales of the Teutonic knights falling through cracks in the ice encumbered by their heavy armor were commonplace, this was most likely a later embellishment by the victors.

The terms Alexander imposed on Hermann were light and quickly accepted. At most the invaders lost 400 men, but the victory was celebrated as the greatest of Alexander's career, and one of the key episodes in Russian military history. Certainly, Alexander ensured that his western border would remain relatively peaceful. The Teutonic Order abandoned any further efforts to invade Rus. After eliminating the threat from the west, Alexander was obliged to turn his attention to the east. In 1246 his father Yaroslav died while returning from the Horde. It is likely that Yaroslav was poisoned by the khan, as execution by poison was one method by which the Horde could eliminate recalcitrant princes who were unwilling to pay tribute. Alexander adopted a policy of collaboration with the Horde while others, including his younger brother Andrey II (1249-52), attempted to rebel against Mongol rule. When Alexander became Grand Prince of Vladimir (1252-63), he continued his policy of collaboration, making several journeys to the khan to convince him of his loyalty. Meanwhile, he repopulated the cities of Vladimir and Suzdal, which were still recovering from the destruction a generation earlier. Alexander died in 1263 and would later be canonized by the Orthodox Church as Saint Alexander Nevsky, the great warrior prince who protected Orthodox Christianity from infidels both east and west.

Chapter 4 – The Rise of Muscovy

When Alexander died, he divided his patrimony between his four sons. The eldest, Vasily, received Novgorod. Dmitry received Pereslavl (a city located 140km southwest of Yaroslavl), where Alexander himself had been born. The third son Andrey was given Gorodets on the Volga, while the youngest, Daniil, became Prince of Moscow. Vasily died in 1271 before he had the opportunity to become Grand Prince of Vladimir, but Dmitry (1277-81; 1283-93) and Andrey III (1281-83; 1293-1304) fought each other for the title. Daniil of Moscow, Andrey's heir, stayed largely neutral amidst his warring siblings and over the course of his reign slowly expanded the territory and population of his relatively poor principality. By the beginning of the fourteenth century, Daniil, now a powerful prince in his own right, was poised to assume the highest title of Grand Prince, but predeceased his brother Andrey by a year in 1303. The Muscovite prince's early death would have major repercussions for the future development of the Russian state.

Daniil was two years old when his father died and made him the first Prince of Moscow, since the city had previously been a minor possession of Vladimir-Suzdal. Moscow first appears on the historical record in 1147 and its founder is said to have been Yury Dolgoruky, the grandson of Yaroslav the Wise, who built the settlement as a strategic outpost on the Moskva River. The city did not escape destruction during the Mongol invasion but recovered over time. The city's central position among the Russian lands protected it from more devastating invasions and attracted refugees from other principalities who sought a more peaceful existence. Although Moscow had risen in status to become a principality under Prince Daniil, it was much poorer than the inheritance enjoyed by his elder brothers. Nevertheless, he was a wise and pious ruler who was much respected by his subjects, and he managed to avoid being involved in his brothers' conflicts. In 1282 he established the first monastery in Moscow, the Danilov Monastery, located at a site around five miles to the south of the kremlin. The monastery continues to be active to the present day and a statue of Prince Daniil stands nearby, erected in 1997 upon the 850th anniversary of the city of Moscow.

Daniil transformed Moscow from a backwater to a powerful principality. In 1302, a year before his death, he inherited the principality of Pereslavl from a childless nephew. However, his death at the age of 42 in 1303 prevented his sons from becoming Grand Prince of Vladimir. When Andrey III died in 1304, the grand princely throne of Vladimir was passed to Mikhail of Tver (1304-18), a nephew of Alexander Nevsky. Mikhail's succession was almost immediately challenged by Prince Yury Danilovich of Moscow, Daniil's eldest son. Yury's actions precipitated a civil war between Moscow and Tver for supremacy among the Russian principalities. This struggle would last more than a quarter century and it was unclear which party would emerge victorious. In the initial stages, Tver enjoyed the upper hand. The city was well fortified and protected by two rivers, the Tvertsa and the Volga, which also facilitated the city's trade. Most importantly, Mikhail was the incumbent and legitimate Grand Prince of Vladimir. The rebel Prince of Moscow was challenging the ruler chosen by the traditional method of succession, and who received his right to rule from the khan.

Yury recognized he was the clear underdog and spent the first decade of his reign in Moscow strengthening his power, conquering Kolomna from neighboring Ryazan, as well as Mozhaisk from the princes of Smolensk. By 1314 he secured the backing of Metropolitan Peter, the head of the Russian Church, and formed an alliance with Novgorod. In 1315 Yury set forth on a journey to Sarai in order to persuade the khan to grant him the yarlyk to become Grand Prince of Vladimir. He stayed at the court of Uzbeg Khan, recently elevated to the supreme office, and over the course of two years engaged in diplomatic negotiations to win the khan's support. Yury was successful in his venture and his alliance with Uzbeg was sealed by his marriage to the khan's sister. Uzbeg Khan formally dismissed Mikhail and appointed Yury to the throne of Vladimir. Mikhail did not accept his dismissal and continued to resist. Despite facing a sizeable allied Muscovite-Tatar force commanded by Yury, Mikhail emerged victorious in battle. Yury fled to Novgorod, but his Tatar wife was captured by the enemy. She soon died in Tverite captivity under mysterious circumstances, causing Yury to claim that she had been poisoned by Mikhail. The khan summoned both warring princes to Sarai to present their cases, eventually ruling that Mikhail was guilty and ordered his execution. Thus, Yury of Moscow became Grand Prince Yury III of Vladimir (1318-22).

The struggle with Tver did not end with the execution of Mikhail at the hands of the khan. Yury's expansionist policies made him an unpopular figure and a target for many rival princes. He had also effectively made himself the khan's tax collector, sending his Muscovite armies to collect tribute for the Golden Horde. Mikhail's sons Dmitry and Alexander continued the struggle and in 1322, Dmitry went to Sarai and persuaded the khan that Yury was siphoning away tribute intended for the Horde. He thus reclaimed the yarlyk and became Grand Prince Dmitry (1322-26). Yury was summoned to Sarai to stand trial for his supposed misdeeds but refused, fully aware that it would likely end in his own execution. Despite these attempts to avoid punishment, in 1325 he was assassinated on Dmitry's orders. Dmitry himself was executed at Sarai several months later for ordering Yury's extra-judicial murder. He was succeeded as Grand Prince by his brother, Alexander of Tver (1326-27).

Yury's younger brother, Ivan Danilovich, continued his brother's policy when he became Prince Ivan of Moscow. He took advantage of a series of altercations between Tatar officials and the princely court in Vladimir which resulted in the lynching of the officials by a mob. Ivan immediately set out to the Horde and persuaded Uzbeg Khan to grant him the yarlyk. The khan was sympathetic to Ivan's cause and sent him 50,000 men to punish Tver. Alexander fled to Novgorod, and then Pskov, where he was welcomed as their prince. Once Alexander found sanctuary in Pskov, the civil war in the Russian lands assumed greater proportions. Faced with a declaration of war from the Golden Horde and most of the Russian princes under the leadership of Moscow, Alexander sought protection from Grand Duke Gediminas of Lithuania. Gediminas had initiated an era of eastward expansion and over the course of his reign (1315-41) conquered major Slavic cities such as Kiev and Smolensk. This was a pivotal moment in the political development of Eastern Europe. Previously the Slavic principalities had been nominally united under the rule of Kiev, and then Vladimir. Lithuania became the largest country in Europe, and its expansion partitioned old Rus between the Golden Horde and Lithuania. In his official Latin title Gediminas styled himself as "King of the Lithuanians and many Russians." Ivan of Moscow (1331-40) may have assumed the supreme title of Grand Prince of Vladimir, but he no longer ruled over the entirety of the Kievan inheritance. Ivan's successors would spend several centuries attempting to take control of all Rus.

Ivan realized that loyalty towards the Golden Horde would best further the interests of his Muscovite state. This policy earned him the nickname "Ivan *Kalita*," meaning "Ivan Moneybags." The khan depended on Ivan and his armies to extract tribute from the other principalities. If the other cities were unable to pay tribute, Ivan used Moscow's wealth to offer them loans, knowing that they would not be paid back. As Moscow's neighboring cities sank further into debt, Ivan sent his armies on punitive expeditions to annex them and enlarge the territory of Muscovy. There are claims that this ruthless policy carried out by Moscow during Ivan's reign inspired the phrase 'Moscow does not believe in tears,' indicating that Ivan's men would stop at nothing to get their hands on the wealth of other cities. The phrase became a common maxim about the city and was the title of an Oscar-winning Soviet film released in 1980.

More than anyone else, Ivan was responsible for the rise of Moscow as the most important city in Rus. He used a portion of his increasing wealth to finance building works in the city. In 1325 he persuaded the Metropolitan Peter to move his see from Vladimir to Moscow, thus establishing Moscow as the religious center of Rus. Moscow was soon made the capital of the principality of Vladimir-Suzdal, even though the title of Grand Prince of Vladimir was temporarily held by a cousin, Alexander of Suzdal (1328-31). In 1326 Ivan built the Cathedral of the Dormition inside the Moscow Kremlin, which would become the most important church in Russian Orthodoxy. In 1333 he built the Cathedral of the Archangel Michael nearby. When Ivan died in 1340, he was buried in this new cathedral, which would serve as the royal mausoleum for Muscovite princes for almost four hundred years. Most importantly, before his death Ivan persuaded the khan to make the succession to the grand princely throne hereditary. This overturned Yaroslav the Wise's succession law which had been in place for three centuries, and ensured that the Grand Prince of Moscow could consolidate his possessions with the knowledge that his sons would inherit his throne.

The change in the succession law paved the road for the centralization of power in Moscow. This process continued under Ivan's sons, Semyon (1340-53) and Ivan II (1353-59), although neither achieved the success of their father. Meanwhile, Moscow continued to be engaged in conflict with Tver. In 1368 Prince Mikhail II, son of Prince Alexander (of Tver, later Pskov), formed an alliance with Lithuania in an effort to reclaim hegemony over the Russian principalities from Moscow. The Muscovite prince, Dmitry Ivanovich (1359-89), a grandson of Ivan Kalita, strengthened the walls of the Moscow Kremlin in anticipation of an enemy assault. During the war Grand Duke Algirdas of Lithuania twice attempted to capture Moscow, but Dmitry's fortifications proved impregnable. Prince Dmitry signed a peace with Lithuania in 1372, and in 1375 he made a favorable treaty with Prince Mikhail, in which Moscow's hegemony over Rus was recognized by the latter. By this stage, Moscow's dominance was recognized by all of the Russian principalities. This display of unity came just in time as Dmitry prepared for a showdown against the Golden Horde.

Chapter 5 – Overthrowing the Tatar yoke

Over the course of Grand Prince Dmitry's reign, the political integrity of the Golden Horde collapsed as princes and warlords fought each other for the title of Great Khan. In the late 1370s, Dmitry seized this opportunity to challenge the authority of the Horde by withholding tribute to the Khan. Dmitry's actions outraged the Tatar commander-in-chief Mamai, who emerged as the leading political figure in the Horde during this period. In 1378 he dispatched an army of 50,000 against the Grand Duchy of Moscow. This army, commanded by Murza Begich, was confronted by Dmitry at the Vozha River. The Muscovite prince decided to fight a defensive battle and stationed his army on high ground. Dmitry and his Muscovite troops occupied the center of a bow-shaped formation, while the flanks were occupied by troops from allied Russian principalities. The Tatars eventually made their move and sought to encircle the Russians on both flanks with their cavalry. However, the Russian infantry provided fierce resistance and the horsemen were unable to successfully execute the maneuver. Dmitry then ordered his men to counter-attack the enemy, whose horsemen were in a state of disorder. Virtually the entire Tatar army was annihilated and its commander killed.

The victory over the Tatars at the Battle of the River Vozha was the first significant defeat inflicted on the Horde by Russian armies. The battle proved to be of great symbolic effect, since it demonstrated that the Golden Horde and its army was no longer the invincible war machine it had been in its early days. The defeat further infuriated Mamai, who in 1380 personally led an army against Moscow despite facing domestic challenges to his authority by rival khans. When Dmitry received news that Mamai was heading to Moscow, he issued a call to arms throughout the Russian principalities and gathered an army at the fortress town of Kolomna, some seventy miles to the southeast of Moscow. On the face of it, Dmitry was a serious underdog. Mamai concluded an alliance with Prince Jogaila of Lithuania who sent a significant force against Moscow. He also had the support of Prince Oleg of Ryazan. Despite the support of the majority of Russian principalities, Dmitry was vastly outnumbered by Mamai's Tatar forces alone. Nevertheless, he decided that his best chance of success was to outmaneuver his enemies and confront Mamai's force on its own. This entailed marching south and crossing the Don River, closing off lines of retreat and condemning his army to destruction if it were to suffer defeat at the hands of the enemy.

The two sides met each other at Kulikovo Field in early September 1380. Early sources provide limited information about the battle and traditional histories of the battle are based on sixteenth century sources which are undoubtedly significantly embellished to establish a grander narrative. According to legend, the battle began with a contest between two champions nominated by each side. As they clashed, their lances ran through the other and both were killed. The two sides then began skirmishing with each other before the main forces clashed. The Tatars and Russians thus came to be entangled in a ferocious melee for several hours as the dead from both sides piled up on top of each other. Dmitry himself was in the thick of the fighting on the front line. He exchanged his armor for that of one of his retinue so he would not be targeted. This did not prevent him from being heavily wounded, while several of his commanders were killed. The Russian line buckled under pressure from the Tatars and was in the process of breaking when Dmitry ordered his reserve, hidden under the cover of an oak forest, into the fray. This changed the course of the battle and the Tatars were soon put to flight. At the moment of victory, Dmitry fainted from loss of blood but survived. He was given the honorific surname Donskoy for his heroic victory. Like his ancestor Alexander Nevsky, Dmitry Donskoy is celebrated as one of Russia's greatest warrior princes.

Dmitry's victory at Kulikovo has become one of the most famous episodes of Russian history. Despite the resounding success of the Russian armies at Kulikovo, the battle did not immediately result in Muscovy's overthrow of the Tatar yoke. The defeated Mamai's authority was significantly weakened and he was soon removed from power and killed by Khan Tokhtamysh, who established himself as Great Khan and reunited the lands of the Golden Horde. In 1382 he embarked on a campaign against Dmitry in an effort to achieve what Mamai had failed to on two previous occasions – the resurgence of Tatar suzerainty over Rus. For the third time in four years, Tatar horsemen galloped across the southern Russian steppes, leaving a trail of destruction behind them, with Moscow as their target. This time, they were more successful and laid siege to Moscow. Although the Muscovite garrison managed to parry the threat through the use of firearms (the first time they had been employed by Russians), Tokhtamysh's Russian allies persuaded the Muscovites to open the gates and promised that the city would be left unharmed. These promises were not honored and the Tatars burned down the city and killed 25,000 people. The sack of Moscow allowed Tokhtamysh to achieve his goal of restoring the authority of the Golden Horde over Rus, as Dmitry agreed to pay tribute as before. Despite the restoration of the status quo, Dmitry's earlier victories set a foundation for his successors to build on as the Golden Horde continued its decline.

When Dmitry died in 1389, his throne was passed to his son Vasily I (1389-1425). Vasily was the first Muscovite prince to inherit his father's titles without the need for the khan's approval. During the initial years of Vasily's reign, the Golden Horde was thrown into political turmoil again as Tokhtamysh turned against his former ally Tamerlane. Tamerlane launched a campaign against the Golden Horde with the intention of restoring the Mongol Empire as it had been under Genghis Khan. In 1395, Tamerlane's armies caused great destruction in the Volga region, sacking cities such as Astrakhan and Azov and weakening Tokhtamysh's authority. Vasily took advantage of these events and released himself from his tribute-paying obligations, ruling as an independent sovereign. In 1399 Tamerlane defeated Tokhtamysh and made his general Edigu the khan of the Golden Horde. After Tamerlane's death in 1405, Edigu launched a series of campaigns against Muscovy. While he failed to capture Moscow, his forces managed to burn parts of the city. By 1412 Vasily was obliged to once again become a vassal of the Golden Horde.

The struggle between Tokhtamysh and Tamerlane during the turn of the 15th century fatally weakened the Golden Horde. Over the course of the 15th century, competing Tatar princes established their own independent dominions, leading to a fragmentation of the Golden Horde. These new entities included the Khanate of Kazan, the Khanate of Crimea, the Khanate of Astrakhan, the Nogai Horde. The remnants of the Golden Horde, which maintained control of the steppe between the Caspian and Black seas, including the capital of Sarai, renamed itself the Great Horde in 1466. The Horde was significantly weakened by the strengthening power not only of the Grand Principality of Moscow, but also the Kingdom of Poland-Lithuania which extended its territories towards the Black Sea. The fragmentation of the Horde did not eliminate the Tatar threat to Muscovy, which was itself engaged in a bitter civil war during the reign of Vasily II (1425-62). In 1439 Grand Prince Vasily was forced to flee from Moscow when it was besieged by Ulugh Muhammad, the ruler of the Kazan Khanate. In 1445 Vasily went on campaign against Kazan but was defeated and captured. The Russians were obliged to pay a large ransom for their Grand Prince.

It was not until the reign of Vasily's son Ivan III (1462-1505) that Muscovy successfully ended its tributary relationship with the Horde. As a young man Ivan fought in his father's campaigns against the Tatar khanates. In 1476, Ivan, as many of his predecessors had done previously, decided to withhold tribute intended for the Horde. Once again, this provoked a Tatar campaign against Muscovy in order to punish the Grand Prince for his insolence. Ahmed Khan launched his campaign in 1480, allied with the Polish king Casimir IV. The Tatar and Muscovite forces confronted each other across the Ugra River, in the same way that Dmitry Donskoy had confronted Mamai across the Don a century earlier. Unlike his illustrious ancestor, Ivan took the cautious approach and did not cross the river. An attempt by the Tatar army to cross the river was rebuffed by the firearms of the Muscovite army, but Ivan did not go on the offensive. For several weeks in October both sides continued facing each other, exchanging shouts and insults, while awaiting reinforcements. By the end of October and the onset of winter, both sides withdrew their forces. In Moscow the withdrawal of the Tatar army was considered a great victory despite the absence of hostilities and the event is known to history as The Great Stand on the Ugra River. The Great Stand came to be seen as the moment when Muscovy had conclusively thrown off the Tatar yoke. However, it is perhaps more appropriate to regard it as a key milestone in a long process during which the Russians strengthened their power at the expense of the Tatars.

The Great Horde was finally eliminated in 1502, although the separate khanates remained in existence for several decades. The Crimean Khanate survived until the end of the 18th century. The collapse of the Golden Horde ended more than two centuries of Mongol-Tatar rule over much of Rus. The so-called Mongol yoke over Rus was far lighter than medieval chroniclers would have us believe. The Grand Princes were given significant political and religious autonomy and it was only when they withheld tribute that the khan launched campaigns of retribution. Nevertheless, two centuries of Mongol rule did have a significant impact on the trajectory of Russian history. At a geopolitical level, the Kievan state of Vladimir and Yaroslav was divided between Poland-Lithuania in the west and Muscovy in the east. This resulted in centuries of conflict between Russia and Poland for control over Rus. Mongol rule over Rus also precipitated the centralization of political authority, not in Sarai but rather in Moscow. The transformation of Moscow from remote backwater to the capital of medieval Rus was the result of Moscow's policy of accommodation and obeisance to the Mongol khan. The military power and wealth which was concentrated in Moscow as a result of the policy allowed her princes to subdue rival principalities over the course of the 14th and 15th centuries.

Chapter 6 – Gathering the Russian Lands

During his 43-year reign, Ivan III not only succeeded in securing the independence of the Russian principalities under Tatar rule, but also in extending Muscovite territory at the expense of the other principalities. The process of consolidating Slavic lands under Moscow's control came to be known as the "Gathering of the Russian lands." As described in an earlier chapter, this process was initiated by Ivan Kalita in the first half of the 14th century and continued under his successors. Despite Moscow's territorial expansion and its status as the leading city among the Slavic lands, states such as Tver, Novgorod, and independent Lithuania retained great wealth and resources and took opportunities to challenge Moscow when the latter was engulfed by succession crises. Ivan III's father, Grand Prince Vasily II, spent much of his reign confronting a challenge to his throne by his uncle, Yury of Zvenigorod, who ruled the Principality of Galich, an important commercial center on the upper Volga. In the process of these wars Vasily was captured by his enemies in 1446 and blinded, subsequently acquiring the nickname Vasily the Dark.

Despite this major setback, Vasily eventually secured victory over his cousins by the 1450s. Due to his blindness, his son and heir Ivan played an active role in political and military affairs and became co-tsar at the end of the decade. Almost immediately upon his accession to the Muscovite throne in 1462 Ivan embarked on a campaign to annex subordinate principalities to the Grand Principality of Moscow. In 1463 he annexed Yaroslavl to his territories, and in 1474 he purchased the lands of the Principality of Rostov. These principalities, although centered on ancient cities, were no longer in a position to rival Moscow. The most important obstacles to Ivan's policy of conquest were the Republic of Novgorod and the Principality of Tver. In 1471 Ivan invaded Novgorod at the head of a Muscovite army, fearful that Novgorod was falling under the influence of Lithuania. The Muscovites defeated a force of 30,000 men and reduced the proud Republic of Novgorod to a puppet state, formally annexing the republic to Moscow in 1478. The proud Novgorodians were unwilling to accept this fate, obliging Ivan order three purges of the city in a decade. The proud city of Novgorod would never recover from Ivan III's brutal policies, though worse was to come.

In 1485 Ivan defeated Prince Mikhail Borisovich of Tver and incorporated his lands into his ever-growing principality. After absorbing the territories of Moscow's rivals and declaring independence from the Tatars, Ivan assumed the new title of "Grand Prince of All Rus," laying claim to the entire legacy of Kievan Rus. Ivan's consolidation of the Russian territories was not the only reason for Moscow's elevated political and religious importance. In 1453 the Byzantine Empire collapsed and its capital was captured by the Ottomans, Islamic conquerors from central Turkey. This event caused shockwaves through European Christendom and led to fears that the Ottomans would overrun Europe. While the Ottoman Empire only reached as far as Hungary at its greatest extent, it made Constantinople its capital and would continue to rule over that city until the empire's collapse following the First World War. Orthodox Christians in Eastern Europe previously looked to the Patriarch in

Constantinople for spiritual guidance. With Constantinople having fallen to the Turks, Moscow remained the most important center for Orthodox Christianity. The monk Filofey of Pskov conceived of Moscow as the successor to Rome. The two previous centers of Orthodox religion, Rome and Constantinople, had fallen to Latin Catholics and Muslims respectively. It was up to Moscow to remain as a bastion of Orthodox Christianity as the Third Rome. While this doctrine was initially conceived in spiritual terms, it would later have political implications. In 1472 following the death of his first wife, Ivan married the Byzantine princess Sophia Palaeologina, the niece of Constantine VII, the last Byzantine emperor. This enabled Moscow to lay dynastic claim to the legacy of the Byzantine Empire.

In order to underline the greatness of his realm, Ivan III initiated an ambitious construction program in his capital city of Moscow. The present-day profile of the Moscow Kremlin dates from the reign of Ivan III. Despite Ivan's wars against Lithuania and his opposition to Roman Catholicism, Ivan cultivated cultural relations with western Europe and hired several Italian Renaissance architects to remodel the Kremlin. In 1475, the Bolognese architect and engineer Aristotele Fioravanti was hired to rebuild the Dormition Cathedral after a previous effort to rebuild the structure was halted after an earthquake. Italians were also asked to work on rebuilding the Annunciation and Archangel Cathedrals over the following decades. During the 1480s, Pietro Antonio Solari and Marco Ruffo remodeled the Kremlin walls, building the distinctive towers that are well-known to visitors to Moscow. Inside the complex the two men collaborated on the Palace of Facets, named after the distinctive rows of diamond-shaped stones that decorate the palace's façade. The palace is the oldest secular structure in the Moscow Kremlin and is now used as a ceremonial hall for the President of Russia.

Ivan III died in 1505 with construction work unfinished. His son and successor Vasily III (1505-33) supervised the completion of the Archangel Cathedral and the Bell Tower of St. John, which was later renamed the Ivan the Great Bell Tower in honor of Ivan III, who was accorded the honorific Ivan the Great during his son's reign. Ivan left to his son a realm three times larger than the one he had inherited 43 years earlier. Vasily continued his father's policies and further extended the territory of Muscovy by annexing the remaining autonomous principalities including Pskov and Ryazan. He also successfully captured the fortress of Smolensk from Lithuania. A descendant of Byzantine emperors through the maternal line, Vasily was the first Russian ruler to officially adopt the Byzantine state emblem of the double-headed eagle. The two heads of the eagle represent imperial dominion over east and west and now serves as the state emblem of the Russian Federation.

When Vasily died he left behind two infant sons, Ivan and Yury. The three-year-old Ivan IV (1533-84) was crowned Grand Prince of Moscow, but political power passed to a council of *boyars* (leading noblemen), who fought each other for political influence. Later in his life, Ivan complained of ill-treatment from the boyars, who were busily fighting amongst themselves and neglected their young princes. The struggle for influence may have been encouraged by the belief that Ivan was a sickly child and was not expected to survive for long, while Yury was deaf and could not be expected to be an effective ruler. Nevertheless, when Ivan reached his majority in 1547, he was crowned "Tsar of All the Russias." This new title was a sign of Moscow's confidence in the international stage. The title *Tsar*, derived from Caesar, had been used in medieval Rus to refer to both the Byzantine Emperor and the Tatar Khan. (The title for the Tsar's wife was *Tsaritsa,* for sons *Tsarevich,* and daughters *Tsarevna.*) While the title had been used in correspondence by Ivan's father and grandfather, Ivan was the first Russian monarch to be crowned as tsar. Through his coronation and assumption of this new title, Ivan IV was laying claim to the legacies of both Byzantium and the Golden Horde.

Once he came to the throne and was able to rule in his own right, Ivan proved to be an ambitious ruler in both domestic and foreign policy. Soon after his accession he established the *Zemsky Sobor* or

Assembly of the Land, an assembly of representatives from three estates: the nobility, the clergy, and the commoners. The body deliberated over a *Sudebnik*, or law code, which was adopted in 1550. The Sudebnik of 1550 was a revision of Ivan the Great's law code dating from 1497, which provided for the centralization of the Russian state by codifying and rationalizing existing legal traditions and extending their authority across the realm. The Sudebnik of 1550 was inspired by Ivan's egalitarian desires, reducing the political power of the aristocratic class which had sidelined him during his youth. Ivan won the support of the common people, who hailed him as a wise and just ruler who prevented aristocratic elites from escaping legal punishments. Ivan's reputation as a champion of the people appears to have been a constant feature of his long reign.

With regard to foreign policy, Ivan first turned his attention to the east. During the early years of his reign, Russia was subjected to frequent raids by the Kazan Khanate. In 1547 Ivan launched a campaign against Kazan but failed to take the city. In order to increase Russia's military capabilities, he established a force of professional soldiers known as *streltsy* or musketeers. In 1551 the Tsar prepared for a second campaign against Kazan. He ordered the construction of a wooden fortress which was floated down the Volga River to Sviyazhsk, some thirty kilometers to the west of Kazan. This fortress would serve as his base of military operations as he led 150,000 men towards Kazan in 1552, laying siege to the city at the end of August. The siege operations were supervised by General Alexander Gorbaty-Shuisky, a young and talented general who was an effective commander. Although the walls of the Kazan Kremlin were formidable, Ivan's army was equipped with siege machines which were operated by Italian siege engineers. By 2 October, Kazan's citadel fell to the Russians, who proceeded to sack the city and massacre its inhabitants. Ivan followed his conquest of Kazan in 1552 with the conquest of Astrakhan in 1556, establishing Russian control of the Volga River. Following his victory over Kazan, Ivan ordered the construction of what is perhaps the most famous landmark in the whole of Russia. St. Basil's Cathedral is situated at the southern end of Red Square. The cathedral consists of nine separate churches, each topped by a colorful dome. The cathedral's official name is the Cathedral of the Intercession. Its popular name derives from St. Basil the Blessed, a holy fool and contemporary of Ivan who was canonized after his death and whose relics are held inside the cathedral.

After Ivan's defeat of Kazan and Astrakhan, Russian political authority began to extend further east. In 1558 Ivan granted a patent to the Stroganov family to colonize Siberia. As wealthy salt merchants, the Stroganovs sought to exploit the commercial potential of the vast expanses that lay to the east of Muscovy. They built forts in order to protect their lands, which were under constant threat from the Khanate of Siberia. In the 1570s they began to hire Cossack mercenaries to defend their estates, who chose Yermak Timofeyevich as their leader. In 1582 Yermak managed to overthrow the Siberian Khanate and capture its capital. Yermak requested reinforcements from Tsar Ivan to consolidate the conquests. When Ivan sent a force of streltsy to Siberia, he claimed the territory for the crown, dispossessing the Stroganovs, and assumed the title of Tsar of Siberia. Yermak was killed in an ambush in 1585, but his legacy of expansion into Siberia was consolidated by Ivan and his successors.

Over the course of his reign Tsar Ivan looked west as well as east. In 1558 he launched a campaign in the Baltic in an effort to establish a foothold on the Baltic Sea, initiating the Livonian War which lasted a quarter century. Although Ivan enjoyed initial successes against the Livonian Confederation – the remnants of the Teutonic Order which had been defeated by Alexander Nevsky three centuries earlier – he was soon opposed by Poland-Lithuania, Sweden, and Denmark. In 1564, Ivan's close friend and advisor Andrey Kurbsky defected to the Lithuanians and participated in military operations in Russia. Kurbsky's defection was a major psychological blow for Ivan, who suspected that other boyars would follow suit. In December 1564 he left Moscow and decamped to the village of Alexandrovskaya

Sloboda without leaving instructions for the government and refusing to respond to any communication from the capital. When a delegation sent from Moscow begged the Tsar to return, Ivan said that the realm was full of traitors and he would only return to the throne if he could be given extra-judicial powers to eliminate them. Ivan's request was granted and he returned to Moscow in early 1565. He duly established the *oprichnina*, a vast region of northwest Russia where Ivan exercised personal rule, supported by enforcers known as *oprichniki*. The policy was notorious for its brutality, but Ivan's actions may be justified by an effort to establish autocratic power and eliminate aristocratic privilege, enforcing the social equality which he legislated for during the early days of his reign. The most notorious atrocity committed by the oprichniki took place in 1570 when Ivan ordered the massacre of thousands of people in Novgorod. The Crimean Tatars took advantage of the political turmoil to launch raids into Russia, and in 1571 set fire to Moscow. In 1572 a 120,000 strong Tatar army marched towards Moscow, but it was defeated by a regular army under the command of Prince Mikhail Vorotynsky at the Battle of Molodi. Ivan soon abolished the oprichnina.

Tsar Ivan IV ended his life a bitter old man, dying in 1584 at the age of 54. Although he had achieved great successes in the east, his efforts to expand his territories westward ended in failure. From 1578, the dynamic King of Poland Stefan Batory launched a series of successful campaigns to conquer the Russian cities of Polotsk and Velikiye Luki. The Russian Tsar, defeated and isolated, made overtures to Queen Elizabeth I of England for an alliance against Catholic Poland, even proposing marriage to the English sovereign. English assistance was not forthcoming and in 1583 Ivan was forced to sign a peace treaty which resulted in the loss of territory to Poland. Although Ivan is known in the English-speaking world as Ivan the Terrible, and the oprichnina appears to confirm this ruthless reputation, the Russian term *Grozny* used to describe Ivan does not carry such negative connotations. It is more accurate to refer to the first Russian tsar as Ivan the Fearsome or Ivan the Formidable. From the moment he assumed the title of tsar at the age of sixteen in 1547, Ivan never ceased to cultivate his image as a formidable ruler.

Part 2 – Imperial Russia

Chapter 7 – The Birth of a Dynasty

As he entered the twilight of his reign, Tsar Ivan nurtured his eldest surviving son Tsarevich Ivan Ivanovich as his successor. During the latter stages of the Livonian War, the relationship between father and son had deteriorated as the young Ivan criticized his father's military strategy. On a November evening in 1581, the Tsar came across his son's pregnant wife wearing immodest clothing and physically scolded her. The Tsarevich leaped to his wife's defense and denounced his father's violence. The Tsar brought up the issue of his son's insubordination during the war and labeled him a traitor. The two men grappled with each other and senior officials rushed to separate father and son. During the confrontation the Tsar struck at his son with his staff, causing the Tsarevich a severe head injury. In an instant the Tsar realized what he had done and cradled the bloodied head of his dying son in his arms. The Tsarevich lingered for several days, but Tsar Ivan's prayers for his recovery were in vain. Although some historians do not believe the Tsar struck the fatal blow, it is the most widely accepted version of Tsarevich Ivan's death.

The unfortunate death of Tsarevich Ivan brought Russia to the brink of a succession crisis following the death of Ivan the Terrible in 1584. Since Ivan and his predecessors had eliminated and dispossessed potential rivals, there were no legally recognized claimants to the throne aside from Ivan's two remaining sons, Fyodor and Dmitry. The 29-year-old Fyodor succeeded to the throne as Tsar Fyodor I (1584-98) but was mentally disabled and did not take much of an interest in political issues. He was a pious Christian and spent much of his time bell-ringing. Tsarevich Dmitry, Ivan's other son, was only two years old when his father died. Moreover, Dmitry had been born to Maria Nagaya, Ivan the Terrible's seventh wife. Under Russian Orthodox law, only the first three wives were officially recognized and therefore Dmitry was widely considered to be illegitimate and excluded from the succession. Consequently, if Fyodor were to die without a son, the Rurikid dynasty which had ruled Rus since the days of Rurik would be extinguished.

The uncertainty over the succession created the opportunity for ambitious boyars to lay claim to the succession in the event of the Tsar's death. During Fyodor's reign, Boris Godunov established himself as the man who held power behind the throne. Godunov had been a leading advisor during the reign of Ivan the Terrible and his sister Irina was married to Fyodor. As the Tsar's brother-in-law, Godunov was setting himself up as the most suitable candidate for the succession. Godunov's path to power was made easier after the mysterious death of Tsarevich Dmitry in 1591. Dmitry and his mother had been sent to the distant Volga town of Uglich in 1584 upon Fyodor's accession to the throne. Godunov claimed the young Dmitry was sent away for his safety, far from the political intrigue in Moscow. Of course, keeping Dmitry far from Moscow strengthened Godunov's own position as a potential successor to Fyodor. In 1591 the nine-year-old Dmitry was found dead with his throat cut. Godunov sent a delegation led by the boyar Vasily Shuisky to investigate the incident. Shuisky reported that the young Tsarevich had been playing a popular childhood game involving a knife, and had an epileptic fit while pointing the knife at himself. Opponents of

Godunov cast doubt on these conclusions. In his play *Boris Godunov* dating from 1836, Russia's great poet Alexander Pushkin supposed that Godunov had hired men to kill Dmitry. In fact, there is no concrete evidence to link Godunov to Dmitry's death. Nevertheless, the specter of Dmitry would continue to haunt Godunov for the rest of his life.

With Dmitry dead, Godunov was the natural successor to Fyodor, who died in 1598. He was duly elected by a specially convened Zemsky Sobor, thus becoming the first ruler of Russia not descended from Rurik's line. As Tsar Boris I (1598-1605), he continued to pursue an intelligent policy of social and economic reform. He continued the centralization of the Russian state and elevated the status of the Russian Orthodox Church. In 1589 he had been instrumental in establishing the Patriarchate of Moscow in opposition to the Patriarch in Muslim-ruled Constantinople. Tsar Boris was interested in the new ideas reaching Russia from western Europe and hoped to encourage their dissemination in his realm. He invited foreigners to Russia to spread western crafts and ideas and was the first Tsar to send young Russian nobles to be educated in western Europe. He pursued a peaceful foreign policy and made commercial treaties with England and the Hanseatic League. For all his intelligent efforts at reforming Russia, Tsar Boris's reign was characterized by tragedy and misfortune, as well as the beginnings of disorder and breakdown of central authority which came to be known as the Time of Troubles (1598-1613).

Three successive years of poor harvests from 1601 to 1603 resulted in catastrophic famine. Government efforts to provide relief to the affected areas were inadequate. The Russian countryside descended into anarchy as bands of desperate men looted villages in search for sustenance. The Muscovites began to wonder whether the famines were the result of divine retribution against Tsar Boris, who had usurped the throne and perhaps ordered the murder of Dmitry. In 1604 an individual in his early twenties appeared and claimed that he was Tsarevich Dmitry. He claimed that he managed to escape

Godunov's plot to kill him and the boy who was killed was a substitute. Despite Tsar Boris's attempts to prove that Dmitry was actually dead, large parts of the country recognized the man as Dmitry and proclaimed him the true tsar. Even leading Muscovite boyars began to declare themselves against Godunov. In April 1605 Tsar Boris suddenly died of illness. He was succeeded by his teenage son Fyodor II (April 1605 – June 1605), an extremely intelligent and learned man for his time, but lacking in experience and legitimacy to exert political authority. In June Fyodor was deposed and murdered, while 'Dmitry' entered the Kremlin in triumph.

It is unclear whether the people of Moscow believed that the man they had placed on the throne was truly Dmitry Ivanovich, the prince who had been declared dead for more than a decade. Russian society at this stage could not conceive of a system of government that did not involve a tsar, and this individual who claimed to be Dmitry merely served as the figurehead of a movement inspired by social discontent. Indeed, soon after the new Tsar was enthroned, doubts resurfaced about his identity. In his manners and dress he resembled a Pole. Furthermore, his court was full of prominent Poles. The Polish presence at court troubled the Russians, who were longstanding enemies of Poland. He was also engaged to a Polish noblewoman, Marina Mniszech. When the couple was married in May 1606, Marina remained a Catholic rather than converting to Orthodoxy, as was the custom for foreign princesses who married into the Russian ruling family. At the end of the month, Vasily Shuisky gathered an army of loyal supporters and marched on the Kremlin, denouncing the Tsar as an imposter who was in fact a Polish monk named Grigory Otrepev. The ruling couple attempted to escape from the pursuing masses, but the Tsar fell and was caught by the mob. They shot him and duly tore his body to pieces. As a sign of their vengeance, they burnt his remains and fired the ashes from a cannon in the direction of Poland. That was the fate of the imposter who ruled Russia for several months as False Dmitry (1605-06).

Vasily Shuisky, the leader of the rebellion against False Dmitry, assumed the throne as Tsar Vasily IV (1606-10). Vasily's authority was limited outside Moscow and he was faced with several challenges. Despite False Dmitry's deposition in 1606, several more individuals claimed to be Tsarevich Dmitry, of which two achieved some prominence. False Dmitry II built a large following of Poles and Lithuanians and defeated an army commanded by Tsar Vasily's brother in 1808. Although he failed to take Moscow, he established a court in the village of Tushino to the north of Moscow. He was "recognized" by Marina Mniszech as her husband, and she bore him a son. In an effort to defeat the rebellion, Vasily concluded an alliance with Sweden at significant cost. The alliance was directed against Poland, which in turn declared war on Russia in 1609. In 1610, Vasily was deposed by an assembly of notables and forced to become a monk – a common strategy Russian rulers employed to remove political rivals. A seven-man boyar council was established to take charge of government affairs.

In an effort to elect a tsar who would be acceptable to all sections of society, a Zemsky Sobor was convened to examine several candidates for the throne. The assembly finally decided on the 15-year-old heir to the Polish throne, Prince Wladyslaw. Given the hostility to Poland and the fact that Russia was at war with the Poles, this choice might seem unexpected. However, there were good reasons to choose a foreign prince. The boyars realized that the elevation of one of their own as tsar would lead to jealousy among the others and prolong the civil war. Thus, they invited Wladyslaw to become tsar on the condition of his conversion to Orthodoxy. Polish troops were invited to garrison Moscow and an embassy was dispatched to King Zygmunt III's court in Warsaw. To the surprise of the Russian boyars, the Polish king rejected the offer. He opposed his son's conversion to Orthodoxy, and he was also intent on conquering Russia's western provinces and annexing them to Poland.

The Polish rejection of the Russian offer prolonged the state of anarchy in Russia. In the absence of a tsar, the Orthodox Church remained the remaining institution capable of inspiring any sense of national unity. Patriarch Hermogenes of Moscow called for Russians to liberate themselves from Polish rule. His sentiments were echoed by Avraamy Palitsyn, a senior cleric at the Trinity St. Sergius Monastery. The statesman Prokopy Lyapunov gathered a volunteer army and successfully recaptured much of Moscow by the summer of 1611, leaving the Polish garrison desperately entrenched in the Kremlin. However, Lyapunov's eclectic army failed to retain cohesion and in July he was killed by disgruntled troops and the army he led disbanded. The cause of national liberation was subsequently taken up in the Volga fortress city of Nizhny Novgorod. A butcher by the name of Kuzma Minin inspired the citizenry with bold words and gathered donations for a Second Volunteer Army. He invited Prince Dmitry Pozharsky, who had served under Lyapunov, to take command of this forces. Minin served as quartermaster of the army and proved to be an able military commander himself. In September 1612 Minin and Pozharsky's army reached Moscow and in October the Polish garrison capitulated.

Minin and Pozharsky's success enabled the restoration of national unity, but Russia remained without a tsar. The Zemsky Sobor reconvened to discuss the question again. The potential candidates this time around were all Russian. The assembly's task was to select an individual who would not alter the existing balance of power between rival noble factions. They offered the crown to Prince Dmitry Trubetskoy, one of Pozharsky's lieutenants who played a major role in the capture of Moscow, but Trubetskoy refused, citing his family's Lithuanian ancestry. The assembly eventually decided on the 16-year-old Mikhail Fyodorovich Romanov. In comparison to families such as the Shuiskys and Pozharskys who could trace their ancestry back to Rurik, the pedigree of the Romanov family was undistinguished. The family name only dated to the 15th century, but its prestige increased when Anastasia Romanova became the first wife of Ivan the Terrible. Anastasia enjoyed a reputation as a kindly woman and was dearly loved by the Tsar. Ivan was heartbroken by her sudden death in 1560 and suspected his enemies of poisoning her. Her brother Nikita continued to play a leading role at court. During the reign of Fyodor I, Nikita's son Fyodor Romanov inherited his father's position at court. When his rival Godunov took the throne, Fyodor was forced to take monastic vows under the name Filaret. During the Time of Troubles, Filaret supported False Dmitry and was appointed Patriarch of Moscow in False Dmitry II's court. In 1610 he was taken into Polish captivity, where he remained when his son was elected tsar in February 1613. The assembly believed they could control the young Tsar Mikhail (1613-45) by obliging him to take advice from the Zemsky Sobor by convening the assembly annually. This arrangement was a long way from constitutional monarchy, but rather an effort by the boyars to reclaim the influence and power they lost during the reign of Ivan the Terrible.

Chapter 8 – The Road to Reform

The election of Mikhail and the inauguration of the Romanov dynasty marked the end of the Troubles. This conclusion is easy to draw with the benefit of hindsight, but it was not so clear to contemporary observers. Tsar Mikhail was a teenager and the unity demonstrated by the boyars in his election could fall apart at any time. The Russians reestablished their authority in Moscow but continued to be engaged in conflict with both Poland and Sweden. The Tsar's father remained in Polish captivity and served as a useful bargaining chip for the Poles. When the Treaty of Deulino was signed with Poland in 1618, Russia paid a heavy price. The ancient cities of Smolensk and Chernigov were ceded to the Polish-Lithuanian Commonwealth. Meanwhile, Filaret returned to Russia and was confirmed as Patriarch of Moscow, head of the Russian Orthodox Church. The Patriarchate enjoyed significant power and resources on its own account, but as a father to the monarch, Filaret effectively ruled Russia on his son's behalf. Upon Filaret's death in 1633, Mikhail ruled on his own account. He summoned the Zemsky Sobor less frequently as he sought to centralize his authority.

Tsar Mikhail died in 1645 after a rather uneventful 32-year reign. In the aftermath of the political turmoil during the Time of Troubles, this may be considered a success. Mikhail was succeeded by his son Alexey (1645-76). The early years of Alexey's reign saw a return to the social unrest that characterized the beginning of the century. Alexey's chief advisor in these years was Boris Morozov, who had served as his tutor. Morozov sought to raise revenue for the state by increasing taxes on a number of goods, including salt. These efforts triggered the salt riots of May 1648, when the inhabitants of Moscow rose up and killed a large number of tsarist officials and demanded the head of Morozov, who managed to escape. Alexey mobilized troops to suppress the uprising, but he recognized he needed to take steps to appease public discontent. He called a Zemsky Sobor to produce a new legal code that updated Ivan the Terrible's Sudebnik of 1550. The new law code, the *Ulozhenie* of 1649, regulated the mass of edicts that had been promulgated in the previous century. The code was a concession to the nobility and townsmen, but it also placed restrictions on peasants' freedom of movement. Thus, the institution serfdom was defined in law.

Alexey's Ulozhenie gave the nobility the sole right to own serfs. This privilege was granted in return for noble service in the Russian army. Over the course of his reign Alexey presided over reforms that improved the fighting qualities of the Russian army. Recent wars against Poland demonstrated that the Russian model of warfare, reliant on quick movements and initiative, was no match for disciplined armies in formation. New regiments of soldiers were formed along western European lines and equipped with imported firearms, which were better quality than those in Russia. These regiments were usually commanded by foreign officers, who drilled the men in line infantry tactics, whereby lines of infantrymen could fire in volleys while advancing and retreating. The majority of western Europeans in Russia came from Germany. A German Quarter was created for these immigrants, both to segregate them from the native population, but also to guarantee them freedom of worship and security from xenophobic conservatives. Following the

English Civil War, Alexey invited scores of Scottish émigrés who fled the country upon King Charles I's defeat and execution. These regiments were employed effectively when hostilities resumed against Poland in 1654. Russia answered the call of Cossack Hetman Bogdan Khmelnitsky, who instigated an uprising against his Polish overlords. The Russian army supported the Cossacks and managed to inflict several defeats on the Polish forces. When the war ended in 1667 with the Peace of Andrusovo, Russia regained Smolensk and assumed control over eastern Ukraine, including the city of Kiev.

The annexation of Ukrainian territories to the east of the River Dniepr (so-called Left Bank Ukraine) encouraged the diffusion of western European learning to Tsar Alexey's Russia. Since Ukraine had been a Polish possession, its religious and scholarly community was familiar with developments in Catholic Europe. Clerics educated in Kiev moved to Moscow to serve in senior ecclesiastical posts. The Tsar's children were educated in Greek and Latin. One of the most important events in 17th Russia, perhaps in Russia's entire history, was the Great Schism of the Russian Orthodox Church. The split came about after Patriarch Nikon introduced wide-ranging reforms to Orthodox worship in 1653. These changes in ritual were on the basis of new interpretations of scripture based on the original Greek text. Among the most controversial changes was the stipulation that the Orthodox faithful should make the sign of the cross with three fingers rather than two. The Church was thus split between the New Believers and the Old Believers. Tsar Alexey supported Nikon's reforms, causing the Old Believers to denounce the tsarist state as heretical. The Old Believers would continue to oppose the Russian state for several centuries.

Although Alexey supported Nikon in his reforms of the Orthodox Church, he came to resent the Patriarch's interference in secular affairs. In 1658 Nikon retired to the New Jerusalem Monastery which he had founded as a replica of the Church of the Holy Sepulchre in Jerusalem. In 1666 Nikon was officially tried by a Church court and removed from office. The power struggle consolidated the Tsar's authority over the Orthodox Church. This development, together with the Nikonian reforms in the Church, weakened the conservativism of the Russian state to some degree. Foreigners living in Moscow's German Quarter were engaged in industry and commerce. The more progressive boyars had their city palaces built in western architectural styles, including the Baroque, which was fashionable throughout Europe. Russian painters trained in the art of icon painting – reproducing images of saints based on popular standards – began to receive instruction from German and Italian artists, who painted portraits of living people. When Alexey died in 1676, he was succeeded by his son Fyodor III (1676-1682). Although heavily disabled and expected to die young, Fyodor was intelligent and continued his father's reforms. In 1682 he sanctioned the establishment of the Slavic Latin Greek Academy in Moscow, Russia's first higher education institution. He also abolished the system of *mestnichestvo*, which ranked families based on their aristocratic lineage.

Fyodor died in 1682 at the age of 21, already surviving beyond expectations. His younger brother, the 18-year-old Ivan, was next in line to the throne and would have been expected to assume the throne. However, Ivan was physically and mentally disabled and even less capable of ruling than his late brother. Consequently, Ivan was passed over in favor of his half-brother, the 10-year-old Tsarevich Peter, who became Tsar Peter I (1682-1725). The decision triggered a political conflict between the families of Tsar Alexey's two wives. Ivan was the son of Maria Miloslavskaya, Alexey's first wife, who died in 1669. Peter was the son of Natalia Naryshkina, whom Alexey married in 1671. The streltsy revolted in support of the Miloslavskys and killed several of Peter's supporters and relatives on the steps of the Palace of Facets in the Kremlin. Eventually, a compromise was reached and both Ivan and Peter would rule as co-tsars, with Ivan V (1682-96) as senior tsar. In reality, since Ivan was incapable of ruling and Peter was too young, political power lay in the hands of Ivan's elder sister Tsarevna Sofia, who assumed the regency.

By all accounts, Sofia was an extraordinary woman for her time. Royal daughters were expected to remain out of sight and secluded in their quarters, effectively a form of secular monasticism. Due to their exalted status, they could only marry foreign princes, but tsars were not always keen to have their daughters married off to foreigners unless there were diplomatic benefits in doing so. Tsarevna Sofia was an intelligent woman who received instruction from the court tutor Simeon Polotsky, a cleric from modern-day Belarus who had studied in Kiev and Lithuania. When her brother Fyodor died, Sofia decided to take an active political role to defend the interests of her family, the Miloslavskys, as well as to avoid the prospect of being secluded in her quarters for the rest of her life. Sofia was assisted by Vasily Golitsyn, a statesman and military commander from a distinguished boyar family. Rumors of a romantic relationship between the two are impossible to prove. In 1687 and 1689 Golitsyn led two expeditions against Crimea, which remained a Tatar khanate as a vassal of the Ottoman sultan. The Russians enjoyed initial successes but ran into difficulties in the arid climate. On both occasions Golitsyn was forced to return to Moscow with significant losses, mainly as a result of disease and starvation. Nevertheless, the armies were greeted with triumphant airs as though they had been victorious.

Golitsyn's "victories" in Crimea fooled no-one. Support for Sofia and Golitsyn's government began to ebb away. By 1689 Tsar Peter turned 17 and reached his majority, leading to calls for Sofia to relinquish the regency and hand the reins of power to her half-brother. Sofia, keen to maintain her family's interests, responded to these calls by seeking to assume the title of Tsaritsa, taking the unprecedented step of ruling Russia as a female monarch in her own name. This step was far too radical for the conservative boyars to entertain. Meanwhile, Peter had taken refuge behind the walls of the Trinity St. Sergius Monastery after being warned of an assassination attempt. Increasing numbers of courtiers and army units left Moscow in the middle of the night and made their way to the monastery, declaring their support for Peter. Peter's supporters duly overthrew

Sofia, who was sent to the Novodevichy Convent in southwest Moscow, where she would remain until her death in 1704. Ivan V remained Peter's co-tsar, and the two half-brothers appear to have enjoyed warm relations with each other until the former's death in 1696. Political power was nevertheless firmly within the hands of Peter and the Naryshkin faction.

Peter had not been idle during his teenage years, when he held the legal title of Tsar but had no political power. Peter and his mother Natalia lived in a palace in the suburb of Izmailovskoe to the northeast of Moscow. Peter was curious by nature and took an interest in many things around him. He enjoyed playing war games with friends and conducted mock battles. He would split his friends into two forces, which over time assumed the names Preobrazhensky and Semenovsky after nearby villages. These regiments were derisively labeled by Peter's superiors as toy regiments, but as he matured Peter was given live ammunition and weapons from the state armory to use in his games. The Preobrazhensky and Semenovsky Regiments would form the backbone of Peter's guard in the early years of his reign. Peter also took an interest in naval affairs and shipbuilding, becoming both a keen sailor and shipwright despite his mother's objections. As an adolescent he often visited the German Quarter, where he would meet with foreign masters and learn their skills. He enjoyed the licentiousness of the district and often indulged himself in drink, a habit which would remain with him throughout his life. Peter regarded several inhabitants of the German Quarter as his close friends. One such individual was Franz Lefort, a Swiss military officer who was a frequent drinking companion. Another was the Scotsman Patrick Gordon, a veteran general who made a major contribution to the overthrow of Sofia's regime. Both men played prominent roles in Peter's early reign as he sought to consolidate power and transform the social, cultural, and political fabric of Russia.

Chapter 9 – Imperial Majesty

Peter's experience in the German Quarter caused him to recognize the benefits of modernization. Russia lagged behind western Europe both in terms of ideas and technology, thanks largely to the conservative influence of the Orthodox Church. During the reign of Tsar Alexey, a small degree of foreign influence could be seen in Moscow. Peter accelerated the process and hoped to transform his people into Europeans in a political, social, and cultural sense. He recognized that western Europeans were more prosperous and lived better lives. Peter believed that in order to be European, his subjects had to dress like Europeans. In the late 1690s, Peter introduced a number of measures regulated fashion at court. The long fur-lined kaftans worn by the Russian aristocracy were phased out and replaced by so-called "Hungarian dress," but which were, in reality, a pan-European style. In an even more radical step, Peter ordered that his courtiers shave off their beards. For Orthodox believers, beards were part of God's inheritance and to shave them off was considered sacrilege. Some particularly conservative Russians may have preferred to have their head cut off instead. Peter allowed exemptions for the merchant community, but they were obliged to pay a tax for the right to wear their beards. In return they were given a token which was inscribed with the words "The beard is a superfluous object." In the case of particularly reticent nobles, Peter would personally take a pair of scissors and cut off a courtier's beard. In another symbolic measure, in 1700 Peter changed the Russian calendar. Russians had previously numbered their years from the creation of the world and the new year was celebrated on 1 September. Peter adopted the Julian Calendar on 1 January 1700 to bring Russia in line with the European powers.

The Tsar realized that in order to achieve his ambitions to make Russia a prosperous country, it needed to be engaged in international trade. The ancient trading entrepots of Pskov and Novgorod, ravaged by war and destruction, were a shadow of their former selves. What Russia needed above all was access to the sea. While Peter had access to the Arctic Ocean at Archangelsk and conducted trade with the Dutch and English from the port, it was far from ideal, since the sea was only navigable for four months in the summer once the ice had melted. At first, Peter looked south to the Black Sea. In 1696 he captured the fort of Azov from the Crimean Tatars. Peter's military engagements brought him into conflict with the Ottoman Empire, the protectors of the Tatars. The Tsar hoped to find military support from the European powers in the war. He set off in 1697 on a Grand Embassy across Europe seeking allies. He visited royal courts at Amsterdam, London, Paris and Vienna, returning in 1698. None of the great powers was particularly interested in an alliance.

Nevertheless, the Grand Embassy was by no means a failure. Peter spent several months in Amsterdam and London learning crafts including carpentry and shipbuilding. Peter managed to master seventeen different skills in his lifetime. The Russian Tsar, although physically a giant at a height of over two meters, was hardworking and modest. He believed that he had to learn manual trades himself if he were to persuade his subjects to take them up. He invited hundreds of craftsmen from all over Europe to Russia in order to teach his subjects.

In terms of diplomacy, Peter's efforts during the Grand Embassy were not entirely in vain either. He established warm relations with Elector Augustus II of Saxony, who was also the elected King of Poland. In 1700 Augustus invited Peter to join an alliance with King Frederick IV of Denmark. This triple alliance hoped to take advantage of the political situation in Sweden, where the young Charles XII had just succeeded to the throne at the age of eighteen. All three powers hoped to conquer Swedish territories in the southern Baltic, and Peter realized that Russian control of the Baltic shore would allow him access to the sea and the potential for lucrative trade links with the rest of the continent. The allies were confident of a swift victory, but underestimated their young opponent. In 1700 After defeating a Danish invasion and forcing Frederick to come to terms by the summer, Charles turned his focus to the Russian army, defeating a far larger force commanded by Peter at Narva in November. The Swedish King then turned to Augustus, who was his strongest member of the alliance. After six years of heavy fighting, Charles was able to remove Augustus from the Polish throne in 1706.

While Charles was embroiled in Poland, Peter reformed the Russian army to prevent a repeat of the debacle at Narva. He labored day and night to train a disciplined, well-armed fighting force. These efforts soon paid dividends as Peter won minor successes in the north, defeating Swedish generals and taking control of the River Neva. In 1703 he founded the city of St. Petersburg on the marshy Neva delta. After defeating Augustus in 1706, Charles XII turned back to Russia. He launched an invasion of Russia in 1709 and met little resistance. Peter ordered his armies to fall back and destroy any supplies that might be useful to the Swedish army. Charles found eastward progress difficult and headed south to Ukraine in an effort to replenish his supplies. He met the Russian army near Poltava and was comprehensively defeated. The Battle of Poltava signaled the rise of Russia at the expense of Sweden. By 1714 a Russian fleet defeated the Swedish Navy at Cape Hango and the Russian army occupied Swedish Finland. When the Peace of Nystad was signed between the warring parties in 1721, Sweden ceded a large amount of territory to Russia. In the peace treaty, Peter referred to himself as "Emperor and Tsar of All the Russias." This new title was taken from the Latin *Imperator* and reflected the western European influence on Peter's rule. Meanwhile, Peter was also granted the honorific title Peter the Great.

Peter's empire was no longer governed from the ancient capital of Moscow but from the newly-founded city of St. Petersburg, where government institutions were transferred in 1712. The city was built on marshland on the Neva delta, several miles downstream from where Alexander Nevsky had defeated the Swedes several centuries earlier. Peter first ordered the construction of the Peter and Paul Fortress on Hare Island. This began as a primitive wooden structure, but was soon rebuilt in stone to the design of the Swiss architect Domenico Trezzini. The fort was constructed in the form of a star, with low ramparts and powerful bastions, inspired by the fortifications built by Vauban, King Louis XIV of France's great military engineer. Trezzini was also responsible for the Peter and Paul Cathedral, a Baroque edifice with a 91-meter spire that remains one of the distinctive features of the city's skyline. Another important institution was the Admiralty, located to the south of the fortress opposite the Neva. This would serve as the base for the construction of the Russian Baltic Fleet, as well for Russia's commercial trade. The Admiralty stood at one end of Nevsky Prospekt, the city's main thoroughfare. The road extended to the Alexander Nevsky Monastery, where Peter transferred the relics of the great warrior saint. Nevsky Prospekt was built by two teams of workers, each starting at one end of the road. When they realized they made an error in their calculations the two sections of road would not meet in the middle, they constructed a wedge-shaped square to connect the two sections.

Peter never envisaged that the Great Northern War would occupy so much of his reign. When the war ended, he made up for lost time by introducing a series of domestic and social reforms. The most consequential of these measures was the Table of Ranks in 1722, which replaced the old mestnichestvo system. Peter aimed to instill meritocratic values into Russian society. He divided offices in the armed forces, civil service, and royal court into fourteen ranks. Everyone regardless of birth began at the bottom and worked their way up the ranks by merit. Non-nobles who reached the 8th rank and above would assume hereditary nobility. Thus, the Table of Ranks was also the means by which Peter reorganized the Russian aristocracy, having abolished the rank of boyar. Although the Table of Ranks would be satirized by Russian political writers in subsequent centuries and many distinguished families soon made their way into the upper ranks, the measure was seen at the time as a radical effort to reform and modernize Russian society. Another measure aimed at encouraging progress was Peter's Church reform. When Patriarch Adrian died in 1700, Peter did not name a replacement. He finally abolished the institution in 1721 and replaced it with the Ecclesiastical College, soon renamed the Holy Governing Synod. Peter effectively established state authority over the Church and named the clerical reformer Feofan Prokopovich as the effective head of the Synod.

Peter died in 1725 at the age of 52. He was buried in the Peter and Paul Cathedral, which would serve as the imperial mausoleum. In his final years Peter changed the succession law to give the Tsar the right to nominate his successor. His eldest son, Tsarevich Alexei, had opposed his father's reforms and died in prison in 1718 after being accused of treason. Peter intended to make his second wife Catherine his heir, and in 1724 staged a coronation ceremony in which she was named co-ruler. However, their relations soon soured when Peter learned of Catherine's affair with a courtier, and by the time of his death Peter did not name an heir. Nevertheless, Catherine succeeded her husband to the throne and ruled as Empress Catherine I (1725-27). The French enlightenment philosopher Voltaire remarked that Catherine's life was even more remarkable than that of her husband. She had been born a peasant in Livonia named Martha Skavronskaya. During the Great Northern War, she was briefly married to a Swedish soldier before being captured by the Russian army and taken as a mistress by Peter's favorite Prince Alexander Menshikov. Peter admired her intellect and beauty, as well as her capacity for drink, and made her his mistress. The two were secretly married in 1707, before a more public ceremony in 1712. When Peter died she was elevated to the throne due to Menshikov's support, though she achieved little during her two-year reign. Nevertheless, there is no doubt that she enjoyed a remarkable and eventful life.

Catherine was the first of several rulers who came to the throne as a result of palace intrigues. Her successor was Peter II (1727-30), the grandson of Peter the Great through Tsarevich Alexei. Aged 12, Peter was too young to rule and political power continued to be exercised by Menshikov, who hoped to make his daughter Maria the bride of the new Tsar. Menshikov unexpectedly fell ill soon afterward. His political opponents at court took advantage of the situation to remove him from power and exile him to Siberia. After Peter was crowned in Moscow in 1728, the court remained in the old capital. Neither Peter nor his nobles wished to return to St. Petersburg. The Tsar fell under the influence of Alexei Dolgorukov, who brokered an engagement between his daughter Ekaterina and Tsar Peter. The couple were due to be married in Moscow on 19 January 1730. However, Peter suddenly fell ill with smallpox and died on the day of his wedding at the age of 15. The Muscovite nobles debated among themselves which of potential heirs they would invite to take the throne. Their choice eventually fell upon Anna Ivanovna, Duchess of Courland, the daughter of Peter's half-brother Ivan V. A group of eight magnates believed that by inviting Anna to the throne, they could extract concessions from her. The offer of the throne included several conditions intended to limit the new monarch's power. Anna accepted these conditions but by the time she arrived in Moscow, she dramatically tore the conditions in half, declaring that she was answerable only to God. The minor nobility supported her position, preferring to serve one rather than several masters.

The reign of Empress Anna (1730-40) has traditionally been characterized as a period of misrule and foreign influence. She returned the court to St. Petersburg, where it remained until 1917. Anna's reign was dominated by Count Ernst Johann von Biron, a Baltic German of modest birth. Biron was close to Anna while the latter was Duchess of Courland and the two are likely to have engaged in a romantic relationship. When Anna became Empress of Russia, Biron was given substantial wealth and enjoyed political power due to his influence over the Empress. He used his position to take bribes and increase his wealth. Russian aristocrats also resented the "German" fashions introduced to Russia by Biron. Meanwhile, Anna herself is characterized as a sadistic and brutal figure with unconventional tastes. This side of her personality was demonstrated by her construction of an Ice Palace to celebrate the wedding between her court jester (a recently demoted nobleman) and an old peasant woman. The couple were invited to spend the night in the palace sleeping on an ice bed. However, despite this characterization, Biron was a competent administrator who stabilized the government amid the palace intrigue, while Anna made significant contributions to the development of Russia's secular culture. She invited Italian composers to write operas for her court and presided over the establishment of a ballet company.

When Anna died, she named as her heir the infant Ivan VI (1740-41), the son of her niece. Ivan was two months old when he became Emperor but his reign lasted a mere thirteen months before he was overthrown by Elizabeth (1741-61), Peter the Great's daughter. In December 1761, Elizabeth led a company of Guards and took power in a bloodless coup, placing her young predecessor in captivity. Elizabeth's reign is associated with profligacy and extravagance. There is no doubt that Elizabeth was a spendthrift. At her death it was discovered that she owned over 16,000 dresses. The Empress' luxurious tastes, no matter how fiscally irresponsible, left a great cultural legacy in St. Petersburg. Her favorite architect was the Italian Bartolomeo Rastrelli, who had already designed several palaces for Anna. Rastrelli's extravagant Baroque style satisfied

Elizabeth's tastes. He was responsible for the design of several of the most famous buildings in St. Petersburg and its surroundings, including the Winter Palace and the Smolny Convent, together with the suburban palaces of Peterhof and the Great Catherine Palace in Tsarskoe Selo. Under the reign of Elizabeth, St. Petersburg became the cultural jewel of Russia and a symbol of Russia's imperial splendor. Elizabeth also presided over the establishment of Moscow State University, which was founded by the polymath Mikhail Lomonosov in 1755. The university remains Russia's most prestigious academic institution.

Chapter 10 – Enlightened Despotism

Elizabeth died on Christmas Day 1761 according to the Russian calendar. At the time of her death, she was engaged in the Seven Years War as part of a Russo-Franco-Austrian alliance against King Frederick the Great of Prussia. Despite Frederick's victories against the odds, by the winter of 1761, the Russian army enjoyed considerable successes and were in occupation of East Prussia. The allies seemed poised to wipe Prussia off the map. Elizabeth's death brought to the throne Peter III (1761-62), Peter the Great's grandson through his daughter Anna Petrovna. Peter was Duke of Holstein and was brought up speaking German before moving to the Russian court. He worshipped Frederick the Great and pursued a pro-Prussian foreign policy, immediately withdrawing the Russian army from the war. This provoked great hostility among the military elite, who were furious that their conquests and sacrifice had been in vain. In the summer of 1762 Peter was removed from power by Guards officers who proclaimed his wife as Empress Catherine II (1762-1796). This time, the overthrow was not so bloodless. Peter was placed under house arrest at Ropsha Palace and died days later. The official notice stated he had succumbed to stomach illness, but assassination is far more likely. In order to consolidate her position, in 1764 Catherine ordered the death of the unfortunate Ivan VI, who died at the age of 24 having spent almost all his life in captivity.

Peter III may have pursued a pro-Prussian policy and behaved as a German, but he was at the very least the grandson of Peter the Great. By contrast, Catherine did not have a single drop of Russian blood flowing through her veins. She was born in Stettin as Princess Sophie Friederike Auguste of Anhalt-Zerbst, and her father served as a general in the Prussian army. In 1744, aged 15, she was taken to Russia to marry Peter, the heir to the Russian throne. She converted to Orthodoxy and took the name Ekaterina Alexeevna. After initial attempts to ingratiate herself with her husband, Catherine soon realized that he was interested in little else than playing with toy soldiers. Unlike her husband, Catherine made every effort to cultivate the affection of the Russian people. She studied the language intensively and demonstrated an interest in folk culture. She conducted several affairs, with Sergei Saltykov, Stanislaw Poniatowski, and Grigory Orlov. Saltykov was rumored to be the father of her son Paul, born in 1755. This seems unlikely, since Paul's character closely resembled Peter III in adulthood. Although Peter had his own mistress in Elizaveta Vorontsova, he was incensed by Catherine's affairs. Rumors that Peter was planning to marry Elizaveta and confine Catherine into a convent – common practice for divorced wives – may have led Catherine to instigate the coup that led to Peter's downfall.

Catherine was influenced by Enlightenment ideas and engaged in correspondence with the philosophers Voltaire and Denis Diderot. She hoped to apply enlightened principles in her exercise of power over her vast empire. In 1767 she established a Legislative Commission to codify the Russian laws which had been introduced since Tsar Alexey's Ulozhenie of 1649. She sent the commission a list of guiding principles known as the *Bolshoi Nakaz* or Great Instruction. The Nakaz began with the declaration "Russia is a European country," reflecting Catherine's efforts to associate her empire with European political and cultural traditions, rejecting the pejorative "Asiatic" label that some western European observers used to describe Russia. Catherine also stated that absolute monarchy was the best form of government in such a vast empire as Russia. The majority of the articles in the Nakaz were copied almost verbatim from the works of the French enlightenment philosopher Montesquieu and the Italian legal reformer Cesare Beccaria. The document was remarkably radical for its time and Catherine's advisers encouraged her to tone down some of the recommendations. The Legislative Commission – representative of almost all sections of Russian society – met in Moscow to deliberate over the issue. The issues were so complex that the Commission could not come to a decision, and Catherine decided to adjourn the sitting of the Commission in 1768. It was never reconvened, and in 1774 Catherine finally abandoned the project.

In the 1770s, Catherine had greater preoccupations than her legislative reforms. In 1773 news of a Cossack rebellion in southern Russia reached the capital. The leader of the rebellion claimed to be the late Peter III, but his real identity was that of Emelyan Pugachev, a Cossack leader. Pugachev recruited a large rebel army, persuading large numbers of serfs to support his cause. During his short reign, Peter III had issued an Emancipation Manifesto which would free the nobility from state service, and peasants imagined that he might also emancipate the serfs. Pugachev promised to end serfdom and taxation for Russia's lower classes. Village priests, even local officers and townsmen joined the rebels as a sign of their grievances against Catherine's government. Pugachev's men won several victories against regular Russian troops and occupied the cities of Kazan and Astrakhan. Catherine realized her empire was in danger. By 1774, the increasing numbers of troops she sent to pacify the rebellion achieved their objective. Pugachev was taken into captivity in September and executed in St. Petersburg in January 1775. The fear of peasant rebellion must have been a motivating factor in Catherine's decision to abandon the Legislative Commission. Nevertheless, Catherine did legislate to grant privileges to the nobles and townsmen. In 1785 she issued the Charter of the Nobility, giving nobles the sole right to own serfs, as well as the right to retire from state service. The same year, she promulgated the Charter of the Towns which gave townsmen commercial privileges. Catherine's failure to produce a similar charter for the Russian peasantry was a major shortcoming of her reign.

In the popular imagination, Catherine has a reputation for taking a series of lovers to whom she granted extraordinary wealth and power. It is certainly true that over the course of her life Catherine had approximately fifteen lovers, but this is by no means an indication of promiscuity. Many of Catherine's male contemporaries would have kept a larger number of mistresses. There is little doubt Catherine's that lovers played a significant role in the political developments of her reign. Grigory Orlov and his three brothers were key players in the overthrow of Peter III. The most iconic of Catherine's lovers was Grigory Potemkin. Their romantic relationship lasted only two years between 1774 and 1776, but Potemkin and Catherine maintained a close friendship until his death. Potemkin held one of the senior commands in Catherine's wars against the Ottoman Empire, alongside Field Marshal Pyotr Rumyantsev and General Alexander Suvorov, who enjoys the reputation of being the most successful military officer in Russian history. Potemkin presided over the conquest of Ukraine and Crimea. Potemkin was named Governor General of Ukraine in 1774, and he founded the cities of Ekaterinoslav (now Dnipro/Dnipropetrovsk), Odessa, and Simferopol. When Catherine visited the area in 1787 it is claimed that Potemkin created fake settlements – so-called Potemkin villages – to give the impression that the cities were larger and grander than in reality. Certainly, Potemkin engaged in some airbrushing to impress Catherine, but the cities which he founded are among the largest and most important in modern Ukraine. His death in 1791 left Catherine heartbroken.

Catherine's expansion of territory in the south at the expense of the Ottoman Empire caused some observers to question her credentials as an enlightened monarch. Another source of criticism was her policy in relation to Poland. Over the course of the 18ᵗʰ century, Russia was in the ascendant while Poland was in decline. In 1764, Catherine engineered the election of her former lover Stanislaw Poniatowski as King of Poland, expecting him to rule as a Russian vassal. These expectations were not realized as Stanislaw proved himself to be an energetic reformer, seeking to strengthen the institutions of the Polish monarchy and reduce the influence of the nobility, which could place major limitations on the King's authority. Stanislaw's reforms caused anxiety among his neighbors. The prospect of a Poland with a strong central authority and a strengthened military threatened the national security of Prussia, Austria, and Russia. In 1772 Empress Catherine of Russia, together with King Frederick the Great of Prussia and Empress Maria Theresia of Austria signed a treaty to partition Poland. Stanislaw was in no position to resist and capitulated to their demands, surrendering a third of his territory. Two more partitions followed in 1793 and 1795 until the state was eliminated from the map of Europe. Some powerful Polish nobles supported the partitions and received guarantees that they could keep their estates.

During the final years of her reign, Catherine struggled over the consequences of the French Revolution of 1789. She initially welcomed some aspects of the revolution since it corresponded with her enlightened principles, which she maintained despite the shortcomings of her reign. However, as the revolution assumed a more radical character, and especially after the execution of King Louis XVI in 1792, Catherine turned against France. She promised to supply 40,000 Russian troops to the coalition which had formed against France, but was preoccupied with affairs in Poland. She argued that the Polish patriots who rebelled against the partitions were part of the same republican movement aimed at overthrowing monarchical regimes. While there were certainly intellectual connections between the French revolutionaries and the Polish patriots, geographical distance prevented them from providing material assistance to each other. Nevertheless, it was a convenient excuse for Catherine not to be actively involved in the anti-French coalition. Catherine also made efforts to crack down on what she considered seditious literature in Russia. In 1790 Alexander Radishchev had written a pamphlet entitled *A Journey from Moscow to St. Petersburg*, where he criticized autocratic rule and highlighted the injustices of serfdom. Radishchev hoped that Catherine would return to her early principles and reinitiate her reforms, but in the context of the French Revolution, she believed the author was inciting revolution and exiled him to Siberia.

Catherine died in late 1796 at the age of 67. Her reforms and her conquests earned her the honorific title of Catherine the Great. Her greatest legacy, however, was as a patroness of the arts. Over the course of her reign she acquired several famed collections of Old Master paintings, which she displayed at the Hermitage, a new building constructed adjacent to the Winter Palace to house her art collection. Catherine was not a particularly discerning collector and she did not have particularly refined artistic tastes, but she made the acquisitions to increase Russia's cultural prestige. The Hermitage is Russia's most popular museum, attracting more than four million visitors every year. Another major cultural achievement during Catherine's reign was the construction of a large equestrian monument to Peter the Great. The vast bronze statue was designed by the Frenchman Étienne-Maurice Falconet and placed on a pedestal fashioned from a single slab of granite called the Thunder Stone, transported from Finland. Latin and Russian inscriptions on the side of the pedestal read "To Peter the First from Catherine the Second," reflecting Catherine's efforts to position herself as the heir to Peter's legacy. The monument is the subject of Alexander Pushkin's poem *The Bronze Horseman*, which serves as a metaphor for the city's grandiose but sinister history.

Catherine was succeeded by her son Paul I (1796-1801). Paul was opposed to his mother's policies and shared his father's passion for military matters. He enjoyed drilling soldiers on the parade ground in front of the Gatchina Palace and dressed his men in Prussian uniforms. He reversed Catherine's policies and dismissed courtiers and generals on a whim, causing the nobility to feel insecure. In 1797 he introduced a new Law of Succession which restored male primogeniture and effectively excluded women from the succession. This is often regarded as a reaction against his mother and female monarchs in general, but the succession law had its merits and largely prevented the palace intrigues which engulfed Russia in the 18th century. Paul imagined himself as a medieval knight in the Catholic tradition, and he accepted an invitation to become the Grand Master of the Order of St. John and sovereign and protector of the island of Malta, which had been occupied by the French and subsequently the British during the French Revolutionary Wars. He ordered the construction of the Mikhailovsky Castle, an imposing fortress around an octagonal courtyard which he believed would provide him with extra security. He moved into the castle in early 1801 before its completion but within a couple of months was overthrown by disillusioned courtiers and generals. Paul refused to abdicate and was killed in the ensuing struggle.

Chapter 11 – Master of Europe

Paul was succeeded by his son Alexander I (1801-25). Alexander's involvement in the coup that killed his father is unclear, but it seems that he sanctioned the insurrection on the condition that Paul would be unharmed. Alexander enjoyed a liberal upbringing under the tutelage of the Swiss scholar Frédéric César de La Harpe, who was invited to St. Petersburg by Catherine the Great. Catherine seemed to hope that her grandson might be able to return to her enlightened reforms when the political climate was more opportune. Catherine seriously considered nominating Alexander as her heir, bypassing Paul, although she died before she could execute these desires. Although he admired and respected his grandmother and sought to please her, Alexander shared his father's passion for the military. Some of Alexander's biographers have suggested that the need for Alexander to please both his father and grandmother serves to explain his contradictory personality, which caused foreign observers to call him the "Russian sphinx." Whatever the truth of the matter, Alexander's reign was characterized by attempts at domestic reform, punctuated by extended periods of war.

Alexander came to the throne as a hopeful reformer. He surrounded himself with a circle of young friends who formed the Unofficial Committee. The most influential member of this group was Prince Adam Czartoryski, a Polish noble who hoped to persuade the Tsar to restore Polish statehood. The Unofficial Committee discussed a range of proposals for social and political reforms. In 1802 the Russian government was reorganized into eight ministries with a cabinet of ministers. In 1809 Alexander asked his chief advisor Mikhail Speransky to work on a proposal for constitutional reform. Speransky's document was presented to the Tsar in 1810 and called for a bicameral legislature, inspired by the British Parliament and the nascent US Congress. The State Council would serve as the upper house and a representative State Duma as the lower house with legislative power. Speransky's plan was only realized in part, as Alexander established the State Council to advise him on political affairs. The Duma was too radical for its time and Alexander shelved the plans. Both the Unofficial Committee and Speransky examined the status of serfdom but failed to produce a realistic plan to reform or abolish the institution. In the 1810s serfdom was abolished in Russia's Baltic provinces, but the freed peasants were given no land and forced to stay on their masters' estates.

Alexander I's reforms did not follow a consistent plan. The primary cause of this was Alexander's shifting political priorities in the context of the Napoleonic Wars. The Russian armies had been actively involved in the French Revolutionary Wars since 1798, when Field Marshal Alexander Suvorov's army won a series of brilliant victories over some of the French Revolution's best generals in Italy. Suvorov's crossing of the Alps into Switzerland in 1799 was a legendary feat, but was precipitated by disagreements between the Russians and their Austrian allies and led to strategic defeat. In 1800, exasperated by the failure of his Austrian and British allies to honor their commitments, Paul switched sides and signed an alliance with Napoleon aimed at British colonial possessions in India. These military ventures were abandoned after Paul's murder in 1801, and Russia and France maintained peaceful relations until 1805.

Napoleon Bonaparte, a swashbuckling general in the French Revolutionary Army, seized power in France in 1799 and ruled over the French Republic as First Consul. In 1804 he crowned himself Emperor of the French in an elaborate ceremony at Notre Dame. Alexander, who held the title of Emperor himself, did not welcome the prospect of the "Corsican upstart" joining the elite club. Furthermore, Alexander had been incensed by Napoleon's orders for the kidnapping and execution in 1804 of the Duc d'Enghien, a French aristocrat who had a claim to the throne. Napoleon's Foreign Minister Talleyrand later remarked, "it was worse than a crime, it was a mistake." These considerations caused Russia to join an alliance with Austria and Britain against France. Napoleon was intent on launching an amphibious invasion of Britain and gathered his Grande Armée on France's western shores. Austria and Russia hoped to take the opportunity to strike in central Europe while Napoleon was preoccupied with his invasion of Britain. However, an effective blockade of the French navy by the British Royal Navy prevented Napoleon from executing his plans.

Even before the defeat at the Battle of Trafalgar in October 1805, Napoleon turned his army east to confront the Austrians and Russians. The allies were surprised by Napoleon's quick maneuvering and an Austrian army was forced to surrender at Ulm, while the Russian army under the command of Mikhail Kutuzov was still marching to its aid. On 2 December, Napoleon defeated the allied army at Austerlitz. Alexander, against Kutuzov's advice, fell into Napoleon's trap by weakening his center and the French counter-attack was devastating for the unsuspecting allied army. Austria soon came to terms with Napoleon but Russia continued to fight as Napoleon turned his sights on Prussia in 1806. The Russian armies did not arrive in time to prevent the Prussians from suffering catastrophic defeats at the Battles of Jena and Auerstedt. In February 1807 Napoleon fought General Bennigsen's Russian army to a standstill at Eylau before a comprehensive victory at Friedland in June. Tsar Alexander decided to come to terms with Napoleon at Tilsit, receiving better than expected terms at the expense of Prussia.

Although Napoleon appeared magnanimous to Alexander, the Peace of Tilsit did involve some serious obligations. Russia joined Napoleon's Continental System, which prevented trade with British ships. Russia and Britain had enjoyed a lucrative trading relationship in St. Petersburg, its aristocratic and merchant community benefitted from the British trade and suffered from the restrictions imposed by the Continental System. By 1810, the Russians intensified secret trade with British ships flying neutral flags. Alexander's failure to adhere to the Continental System incensed Napoleon, who began planning for the resumption of hostilities with Russia. Alexander was equally aware that the outbreak of hostilities may be imminent, and appointed General Mikhail Barclay de Tolly as Minister of War in 1810. Barclay de Tolly was a Baltic German officer of Scottish descent who had proven himself as a capable administrator and military thinker in earlier engagements. He embarked on a series of reforms to improve the fighting capabilities of the Russian army and developed war plans in the event of Napoleon's invasion.

In June 1812 Napoleon invaded Russia with 500,000 men. He sent detachments towards St. Petersburg and Ukraine, but his main force was directed at Moscow. Barclay was appointed commander-in-chief of the 120,000 strong First Western Army and assumed de facto command of the entire army. Prince Pyotr Bagration's Second Western Army of 40,000 men was also deployed on Russia's western borders, but Barclay recognized that he could not fight when outnumbered to such a great extent. Accordingly, Barclay pursued a defensive scorched earth campaign, drawing Napoleon's armies deeper into the heart of Russia. However, Barclay's strategy opposed by Bagration and much of the Russian command. After abandoning the city of Smolensk to Napoleon after a fierce two-day battle, Barclay was superseded in command by Field Marshal Kutuzov. Kutuzov fought an impressive battle against Napoleon at Borodino at the end of August, but was forced to fall back. At a council of war in the village of Fili outside Moscow, Kutuzov made the fateful decision to abandon Moscow to Napoleon. The conqueror sat in the Kremlin expecting Alexander to come to terms, but the Russian monarch refused to answer Napoleon's letters. Meanwhile, Moscow was set on fire – either purposefully or accidentally – preventing the Grande Armée from taking up winter quarters. Once the snow began to fall in October, Napoleon was forced to abandon Moscow to search for supplies in the fertile south.

Kutuzov's army intercepted Napoleon's march at Maloyaroslavets and forced him to turn back. The images of the remnants of the Grande Armée succumbing to the bitter cold of the Russian winter are a familiar feature of the 1812 campaign. The Russian army continued its pursuit of the French into 1813. Kutuzov liberated a host of German and Polish cities from French rule but succumbed to illness and died in May 1813, succeeded eventually by Barclay de Tolly. Meanwhile, Alexander employed his considerable diplomatic charm to persuade Prussia and Austria to join an alliance aiming to overthrow Napoleon. The allies formed three major armies: the Army of Bohemia under the command of Austrian Field Marshal Karl Philipp von Schwarzenberg, Prussian Field Marshal Gebhard Lebrecht von Blucher's Army of Silesia, and the Army of the North under the command of Crown Prince Karl Johann of Sweden, who had previously served in Napoleon's army as Marshal Jean Bernadotte. While the French Emperor demonstrated considerable tenacity, he was considerably outnumbered by the allies and was defeated at the Battle of Leipzig in November 1813. By the following spring, the coalition armies flooded over the eastern borders of France and captured Paris. Napoleon's marshals advised him to abdicate the throne. After futile efforts at resistance, Napoleon signed the abdication and was exiled to the Mediterranean island of Elba. Louis XVIII, brother of the executed Louis XVI, became King of France.

As the coalition armies conquered their way through Europe, Alexander joined the armies on campaign together with Emperor Franz I of Austria and King Friedrich Wilhelm III of Prussia. In addition to discussions about military strategy, the monarchs deliberated over the future of Europe. These debates were formalized with the Congress of Vienna, which opened in the Austrian capital during summer of 1814. The key players during the Congress were Austria, Russia, Prussia, Britain, and France, represented by Talleyrand, who became Louis XVIII's Foreign Minister. Alexander aimed to present himself as a magnanimous victor and did not wish to punish France. He also favored a liberal constitution in France to prevent it from to succumbing to revolution once again. However, Alexander's objectives were not completely altruistic and he laid claim to the entirety of Poland. The Tsar hoped to restore Polish statehood under Russian influence, but the Prussians and Austrians were uneasy about the westward projection of Russian power. Disputes over the future of Poland led to threats of war between the negotiating powers. Only when Napoleon escaped from Elba and was welcomed back in France did the powers at Vienna renew their alliance. The Duke of Wellington and Blucher's victory at the Battle of Waterloo in June 1815 forced Napoleon's second abdication. This time, he was exiled to the distant island of Saint Helena in the south Atlantic, where he would die in 1821. The Congress finalized its business at the end of 1815, resulting in a set of compromises between the great European powers. Russia was granted a significant part of Poland which would become the Kingdom of Poland, but others remained under Prussian and Austrian rule.

After the Napoleonic Wars Alexander's rule assumed a more conservative character, although efforts at reform continued. He granted Poland a constitution, and in 1818 he asked his advisor Nikolay Novosiltsev to produce proposals for a constitution for Russia, though nothing came of the project. As part of the effort to demobilize the army, Alexander embarked on a disastrous military colonies reform. This would keep soldiers stationed in colonies situated in strategic positions, and in peacetime they would be expected to work the land. Peasants from neighboring areas would replenish the colonies over time. Thus, soldiers were expected to become peasants and peasants expected to become soldiers. Neither group favored the arrangement and the policy was gradually abandoned. Alexander died in 1825 in the southern port city of

Taganrog. The circumstances of his death are unclear, and some theories suggest that Alexander faked his death in order to quietly relinquish the throne. In the 1850s Siberian holy man named Fyodor Kuzmich appeared in Omsk and was identified with the Tsar, and subsequent generations of the Romanov family were brought up to believe that Tsar Alexander and Fyodor Kuzmich were the same person.

The true circumstances of Alexander's death may never be explained, but the Russian throne was left vacant in December 1825. Alexander's heir was his younger brother Constantine, who ruled as Governor General of Poland. However, Constantine had married a Polish noblewoman and refused the succession, leaving younger Grand Duke Nicholas next in line. When Alexander died, Nicholas was not aware of Constantine's refusal and swore an oath of loyalty to his elder brother, only for Constantine to publicly renounce the throne. Eventually, Nicholas agreed to assume power himself. In the political turmoil that ensued, a group of radical and liberal officers refused to swear an oath to Nicholas, shouting "Constantine and Constitution." Nicholas was unwilling to give orders to suppress the rebellion, fearing that his orders to kill fellow Russian soldiers would not be obeyed. In an effort to diffuse the situation, Nicholas sent General Mikhail Miloradovich, Governor of St. Petersburg and a hero of the Napoleonic Wars, to talk to the rebels. A rebel officer named Pyotr Kakhovsky shot Miloradovich and killed him. Nicholas then ordered loyal troops to fire their cannons at the rebels, inflicting terrible casualties and dispersing the rebels. Five leaders of the so-called Decembrist Rebellion were executed by hanging. Another hundred or so were sent into Siberian exile.

Chapter 12 – Reform and Reaction

Tsar Nicholas I (1825-55) assumed the throne in inauspicious circumstances. The military justice and draconian punishments issued by Nicholas in the aftermath of the Decembrist Uprising foreshadowed his 30-year reign. Nicholas's rule was encapsulated by the slogan "Orthodoxy, Autocracy, Nationality," devised by Minister of Education Sergey Uvarov in 1830. Nicholas's commitment to Russian nationalism was reflected in the brutal suppression of a Polish uprising in 1830 which led to the removal of Poland's constitutional privileges. More than any other Russian ruler, Nicholas was the embodiment of Russian autocracy. He concentrated power into His Majesty's Own Chancellery, whose officers were directly responsible to the Tsar. The work of Nicholas's Chancellery had some positive outcomes. The Second Section was responsible for legislation and headed by Mikhail Speransky, Alexander I's former chief secretary who had been exiled to Siberia in 1812. Speransky gradually returned to favor and as Governor of Siberia successfully reorganized the regional government of the vast territory. Nicholas invited him back to St.

Petersburg to preside over the codification of Russia's laws. This monumental task was completed in 1830. An edited collection of 46 volumes appeared in 1835 and served as Russia's primary legal code. The more notorious element of the Chancellery was its Third Section, responsible for policing and security. Under the leadership of Alexander Benckendorff, the Third Section monitored the empire for political dissent. Liberal opponents of the regime such as Alexander Herzen described Russia under Nicholas as a police state.

Despite the sinister nature of his political rule, Nicholas's reign also coincided with the Golden Age of Russian literature. Alexander Pushkin continues to be regarded as the greatest Russian writer of all time. Pushkin had written radical verses in his youth and was banished from St. Petersburg. From exile in southern Russia and later at his mother's estate of Mikhailovskoye, Pushkin began writing *Eugene Onegin*, a tale of unrequited love which served as a critique of Russian aristocratic society. Pushkin was investigated for his connections to the Decembrist Uprising – many of the leaders were close friends – but escaped punishment. Tsar Nicholas fully recognized Pushkin's literary genius and allowed him to return to St. Petersburg. In order to temper the poet's radicalism, the Tsar acted as Pushkin's personal censor. Pushkin was more than a poet, and his literary output also includes prose and history. In 1836 he was appointed court historiographer by the Tsar and given access to the imperial archives to write a history of Peter the Great, but was killed in a duel soon after. Pushkin's untimely death in 1837 remains a great tragedy for Russian literature. Other literary luminaries of the era included Mikhail Lermontov and Nikolay Gogol. Gogol's short stories *The Overcoat* and *The Nose* played on the absurdity of the St. Petersburg bureaucracy. His play *The Government Inspector* satirized provincial bureaucrats as they fell over themselves to flatter officials from St. Petersburg. Although the conservative press criticized the play, Nicholas intervened to have it staged and enjoyed the performance. Corrupt imperial officials rendered the Tsar's government less efficient and Nicholas appreciated satire directed against lower-ranking officials.

Nicholas's conservatism at home was also reflected in his foreign policy. In the aftermath of the French Revolutionary and Napoleonic Wars, the great powers of Europe – especially Austria, Prussia, and Russia, aimed to suppress nascent national revolutionary movements. As imperial entities, Russia and Austria were keenly aware of the threat of national revolutions to their territorial integrity. In 1830 Nicholas brutally suppressed a Polish uprising and brought the Polish state under direct rule. He was reluctant to support the Greeks in their War of Independence from the Ottoman Empire, only doing so in the latter stages of the conflict. Nicholas was instrumental in the suppression of the revolutions of 1848 which engulfed the continent. The Austrian Habsburgs were faced with national uprisings in Italy and Hungary. The Hungarian revolutionaries managed to defeat Austrian attempts to suppress resistance and in 1849 established a government led by Lajos Kossuth. The new Habsburg Emperor Franz Josef I was obliged to request military support from his Russian counterpart. Tsar Nicholas obliged and the combined Austro-Russian army successfully suppressed the uprising.

Nicholas's reactionary foreign policy earned him the nickname "the gendarme of Europe." During the reign of Nicholas, the Russian Imperial Army continued to enjoy the reputation of Europe's most powerful army due to its contribution to the defeat of Napoleon. In 1853 Nicholas invaded the Ottoman provinces of Wallachia and Moldavia, threatening to upset the European balance of power. The Tsar hoped that his army's formidable reputation would deter Russia's rivals from intervening in the conflict. These expectations were not realized and in 1854 Britain and France formed an alliance with the Ottomans to resist Russia. Crucially, Austria, which had recently been the beneficiary of Russian military assistance and was expected to support Russia, remained neutral. The British and French invaded Crimea and occupied several strategic positions on the island. The Russians fought bravely in defense of their stronghold at Sevastopol, but the besieging British and French forces finally took the port city in September 1855. Meanwhile, mentally and physically broken by reports of military setbacks in Crimea, Tsar Nicholas died in February 1855. His son Alexander II succeeded to the throne and sued for peace in the spring of 1856.

Tsar Alexander II (1855-81) recognized that defeat in Crimea was a national humiliation. In order to restore Russia's military capabilities, not only the army but the whole of Russian society had to be reformed. Britain and France were industrialized economies and had access to technologically advanced weaponry. Moreover, the British and French soldiers enjoyed political and civil rights and shared a sense of nationhood, while Russian rank-and-file soldiers were peasants with no great attachment to national issues. Alexander enjoyed a liberal upbringing under the tutelage of Vasily Zhukovsky, a romantic poet and close friend of Pushkin. In order to signal his liberal credentials, soon after his accession Alexander II granted an amnesty to the surviving Decembrist exiles in Siberia, enabling them to return to their homes and restoring their property. Alexander also believed that serfdom had to be abolished in order to stimulate agricultural and industrial activity. The Russian nobility was vehemently opposed to the abolition of serfdom since much of their wealth was tied up in serfs. In a speech to an assembly of nobles in Moscow in 1856, Alexander warned his audience that if the state did not emancipate the serfs from above, the serfs would emancipate themselves from below. Nevertheless, it took several years to establish the terms of the Emancipation Manifesto, which was announced by the Tsar in March 1861. The chief architect of Alexander's emancipation policy was Deputy Minister of Justice Nikolay Milyutin. A liberal reformer, Milyutin hoped to grant the emancipated serfs the land which they worked on. However, the nobles did not wish to relinquish the land without compensation and eventually the state agreed to buy the land from the nobles. The freed serfs were obliged to pay redemption dues to the state for a period of 49 years. Although news of the emancipation was welcomed with euphoria across much of the country, this soon turned into anger and dissatisfaction once the peasants realized the scale of their financial obligations to the state.

In addition to the emancipation reform, which earned him the nickname of Tsar-Liberator, Alexander embarked on political and judicial reforms in Russian towns and the countryside. Now that the serfs became free peasants, the Tsar reformed local political institutions in order to give them political rights. In 1864 Alexander introduced representative village councils known as *zemstva*, which included representation from the peasantry. These new bodies were given extensive powers over taxation and issues such as education, healthcare and public welfare. Over the following decade they were introduced across the country. In 1870 trial by jury was introduced in lower courts throughout the empire. This was a major departure from the traditional judicial institutions which were controlled by the nobility. Alexander's jury system included a radical and unique feature whereby juries could decide that a defendant was guilty of a crime without applying any punishment. This was a major departure from the reign of Nicholas I when the letter of the law was supreme. Unlike the emancipation and zemstva reforms which were criticized for their inconsistency and unintended consequences, Alexander's jury reforms are widely regarded as a success and a significant improvement on the previous system of justice.

Although Alexander cultivated the image of a great reformer, he was criticized by radical and liberal intellectuals for pursuing half-hearted reforms. The emancipation settlement imposed a heavy financial burden on the peasants. Political and judicial reforms did not extend to the higher state organs. Alexander had no plans to introduce a constitution to limit his autocratic power. As a result, radical political groups continued to oppose the Tsar and made plans to overthrow the tsarist regime. Over the course of his reign Alexander was the target of seven assassination attempts. The first attempt was carried out by Dmitry Karakozov in April 1866, who blamed the Tsar for the suffering of the workers and the urban poor. The Tsar escaped unharmed, but the incident shocked Russian society. Russian monarchs had been assassinated before, but only in the context of palace intrigues hidden from public view. Karakozov's attempt was the first time a public assassination attempt had taken place. Alexander would survive five more assassination attempts but his luck ran out on 1 March 1881. The Tsar was returning from a routine military inspection traveling inside a bulletproof carriage when a bomb was thrown at the imperial vehicle by a member of the terrorist group People's Will. Alexander was unharmed but the explosion had killed one Cossack and injured many others. He instructed the driver to return to the spot of the explosion and stepped out of his carriage. At that moment another assassin threw a bomb at the Tsar's feet, shattering his legs. The mortally wounded sovereign was taken back to the Winter Palace, where he died not long after.

The murdered Tsar's son and successor, Tsar Alexander III (1881-94), did not expect to assume the imperial mantle. His elder brother, Tsarevich Nikolay Alexandrovich, had been brought up as a liberal by Alexander II and was seen as Russia's great hope. In 1865, Nikolay suddenly fell ill and died, leaving his younger brother Alexander as heir. Alexander received little political education and the law professor Konstantin Pobedonostsev was engaged to instruct the heir in political administration. Pobedonostsev was an initial supporter of Alexander II's reforms, but his political views became more conservative over time. In the latter years of his father's reign, Tsarevich Alexander would emerge as the spokesman for the conservative opposition to Alexander II's reforms. When Alexander III assumed the throne, he pursued a nationalist policy. He was physically imposing and looked like a Russian peasant, despite being 99 percent German. His strength was legendary and at state dinners he would bend cutlery out of shape with his bare hands as a demonstration of Russian power to foreign diplomats. When he became Tsar, Alexander issued a manifesto which ended Alexander II's reforms. The powers of the zemstva were reduced, and noble land captains were introduced to preside over peasant communes. Universities became the subject of greater scrutiny as students were especially prone to espousing revolutionary doctrines. Alexander also presided over a crackdown of terrorist groups such as the

People's Will. Nevertheless, radical revolutionary parties continued to operate underground.

Although Alexander's reign is associated with reactionary domestic policies, he did preside over reforms which led to accelerated industrialization and modernization of the Russian economy. These reforms are usually associated with Sergei Witte, who served as Minister of Finance between 1892 and 1903, but were initiated by his predecessor Ivan Vyshnegradsky. Witte encouraged foreign investment into Russia, which funded large infrastructure projects such as the Trans-Siberian Railroad. This project was especially close to Witte's heart, as he had served as Minister for Railways and previously worked in the railroad industry. Most of the funding for the project came from France, which in 1894 signed an alliance with Russia in response to the expansion of the German Empire. The railroad would facilitate the mobilization of Russian troops from the depths of Russia to its western frontiers. As a result of these industrial developments, Russian GDP grew by an average of 10 percent per year during the 1890s. However, industrialization during Alexander III's reign came at a significant cost to the peasantry. Witte's industrialization was funded not only by foreign investment but also by increased taxation on the peasantry, who were already burdened with redemption dues. The Russian countryside experienced desperate famine at the beginning of the 1890s and incidents of peasants rising up against their landowners and burning their estates were not uncommon during the period. Although Alexander III's diplomatic ventures earned him the nickname The Peacemaker, he was to bequeath a fracturing empire to his son Nicholas upon his early death in 1894.

Chapter 13 – War and Revolution

Like his father, Tsar Nicholas II (1894-1917) was unprepared for the duties of Emperor of Russia when he came to the throne. Unlike his father, Nicholas was the eldest son and expected to inherit the throne. However, while Nicholas received a good education and was an intelligent man who mastered several languages, he was not invited to the deliberations of his father's Council of Ministers. Alexander III may have expected to reign for at least another twenty years, during which his son would gradually be introduced to matters of state, but he died in 1894 at the age of 49. Unlike his father, who exhibited a harsh and stern demeanor, Nicholas's was compassionate and sentimental by nature. Nevertheless, he would continue his father's reactionary nationalist policies in an effort to maintain his authority, which he believed to have been given to him by God. Nicholas's reign did not begin auspiciously. Shortly before the death of his father, Nicholas was engaged to Princess Alix of Hesse, who would become Empress Alexandra Fyodorovna. The wedding took place almost immediately after the end of the mourning period for the late Tsar Alexander. The shift from mourning to celebration seemed too abrupt and the royal couple were criticized for hurrying to the altar. More ominous were the circumstances of Nicholas's coronation in 1896. A large celebration had been planned at Khodynka Field to the northwest of Moscow, where a crowd of 500,000 people gathered in anticipation of receiving gifts from the Tsar. There was a panic that there would not be enough gifts to go around, resulting in a stampede which caused the deaths of more than a thousand people. The bloody start to Nicholas II's reign foreshadowed a bloody end.

Nicholas came to the throne at a time when there was significant opposition to the tsarist system of political rule in Russia. His grandfather Alexander II had been assassinated by terrorists, and terrorist attacks continued to claim the lives of imperial officials throughout the country despite Alexander III's best attempts to eliminate political opposition. Three distinct political groups emerged during the 1890s. The liberals, including Pavel Milyukov and Alexander Guchkov, called for social reform, economic modernization, and constitutional government. They did not pursue violent methods but aimed to persuade decision makers through the press. The populists, who would form the Social Revolutionary Party (SRs) in 1902, catered to Russian peasants and espoused agrarian socialism, favoring the redistribution of noble land to the peasantry. Radical elements of the SRs carried out extensive campaigns of political violence throughout the country. Led by Viktor Chernov, the SRs were by far the most popular political party in Russia during the turn of the twentieth century. The final group were the Social Democrats (SDs), who were influenced by Marxist political theory and aimed to mobilize the urban proletariat to overthrow the tsarist regime. Key leaders of the Social Democrats included Georgy Plekhanov, Julius Martov, and Vladimir Lenin.

The political opposition to Nicholas looked for an opportunity to strike at the heart of the tsarist political system. On Sunday 9 January, a group of striking workers embarked on a procession to the Winter Palace to register their grievances to the Tsar about the behavior of factory owners. The workers carried religious icons and images of Tsar Nicholas and sang Orthodox hymns, including the imperial anthem *God Save the Tsar*. This was far from a revolutionary act, but a traditional procession of loyal petitioners who believed their father-tsar would intercede on their behalf. On the day of the march, Nicholas was absent from the Winter Palace and was staying at the Alexander Palace in Tsarskoe Selo. When the march was underway, the soldiers tasked with keeping order appear to have been intimidated by the size of the procession and began to fire. Many accounts describe the soldiers as Cossacks, but in fact most of them were soldiers of the elite Preobrazhensky Guards. In total, around 1000 men, women and children were killed, both from the initial rifle fire and the stampede that followed as the demonstrators fled from the scene. The events of Bloody Sunday sparked a series of strikes across the city which threatened to topple the government. Public confidence in Nicholas's rule was also diminished by setbacks in the Russo-Japanese War, which had been launched in 1904 to consolidate Russian colonial possessions in Manchuria and the Korean Peninsula. In May 1905, the Russian Baltic Fleet, which had made its way halfway around the world and was renamed as the Second Pacific Fleet, suffered a catastrophic defeat at the Battle of Tsushima. This was soon followed by a famous mutiny onboard the *Potemkin*, a battleship of the Black Sea Fleet.

As St. Petersburg was in the grip of political turmoil, liberal elements in Russian society attempted to persuade the Tsar to grant political concessions including a constitution and workers' rights. Nicholas responded that he would not grant a constitution under any circumstances. He seemed to be keenly aware of his lack of aptitude for political leadership and proposed that his uncle Grand Duke Nikolay Nikolayevich be appointed military dictator to suppress the revolution. When the Grand Duke responded to the offer by telling the Tsar that he would rather shoot himself, Nicholas II had no other choice but to introduce the October Manifesto, which would result in the establishment of the State Duma, an elected legislative assembly which would vote on new laws. These measures were enacted in

April 1906, inspired by Speransky's constitutional reform plans a century earlier. Radical deputies were elected to the Dumas, and they voted down the vast majority of the proposed laws. As a result, the first two sessions were quickly suspended and new elections called. The electorate was reduced for the elections to the Third Duma, resulting in a majority for conservative parties, including the Octobrist Party led by Alexander Guchkov. Guchkov maintained a close working relationship with Prime Minister Pyotr Stolypin and assisted reforms to the Russian agrarian economy between 1906 and 1910. The parliamentary experiment appeared to be working and enabling reform, but Stolypin fell out of favor in 1910 and was assassinated the following year.

Although Nicholas was confronted with many domestic political problems, by the 1910s foreign policy assumed greater importance in the political agenda. The Balkan Wars of 1912 and 1913 created tensions between Russia and Austria-Hungary. Russia supported the independence of the Orthodox nations in the Balkan peninsula while the Austrians hoped they would remain part of the Habsburg empire. When Archduke Franz Ferdinand of Austria-Hungary was assassinated in late June 1914, it brought Austria into conflict with Serbia, a Russian ally. The rival European alliances at the time brought the rest of Europe into the conflict, leading to the outbreak of the First World War in August. Although the Russian armies mobilized rapidly, it was ill-equipped and defeated comprehensively by German armies under the command of Generals Paul von Hindenburg and Erich Ludendorff at Tannenberg and the Masurian Lakes. The Russians were forced to fall back several hundred miles to more defensible positions and Nicholas decided to assume personal command of the army. This decision may have bolstered the war effort, but contributed to political disorder in the capital, which was renamed Petrograd. Despite the initial successes of General Alexey Brusilov's offensive against the Austrians in the summer of 1916, the political situation in the home front continued to deteriorate as efforts by civil society to support the war effort were undermined by the government as it sought to maintain its autocratic power. The liberal leader Pavel Milyukov charged the government with treason or incompetence in its mishandling of the war effort.

In early 1917, hundreds of thousands of workers went on strike and staged demonstrations in Petrograd demanding better pay and working conditions. By February, the crisis threatened to overwhelm the government. The regime attempted to suppress the demonstrations by force but some regiments mutinied and joined the workers on the streets. Even the elite Preobrazhensky Guards defied their officers and raised the red banner of revolution. Nicholas failed to appreciate the danger of the situation until it was too late. He attempted to return to Petrograd from army headquarters, but the imperial train was stopped en route by striking railroad workers and forced to divert to Pskov. There he was met by leading politicians and generals who advised him to abdicate. Eventually, Nicholas decided to sign the abdication but nominated his brother Mikhail rather than his hemophiliac son Alexey as successor. Mikhail was enthusiastic about the prospect of becoming a constitutional monarch, but was persuaded to decline the throne until a Constituent Assembly could meet to decide on Russia's future. This effectively spelt the end of the Romanov dynasty, which had ruled Russia for 304 years.

Even before news of the Tsar's abdication reached Petrograd, a group of Duma politicians established a new government. It called itself the Provisional Government since it would take charge of day-to-day administration until the Constituent Assembly could meet at the end of the year. The Provisional Government was led by Prince Georgy Lvov and dominated by liberals, with Pavel Milyukov and Alexander Guchkov serving as Foreign Minister and War Minister respectively. Despite the fact that the workers on the streets were mainly socialists, Minister of Justice Alexander Kerensky was the only socialist minister in the Provisional Government. Kerensky also happened to be Deputy President of the Petrograd Soviet, a body representing workers and soldiers and dominated by socialist parties.

The Soviet exercised a lot of unofficial power and effectively shared power with the Provisional Government. The army would only execute orders from the Provisional Government if they were sanctioned by the Soviet. This phenomenon of Dual Power hindered the government's ability to resolve the social and economic problems which led to the revolution. Nevertheless, the Soviet opted to support the Provisional Government, and many of its leading figures would also take up ministerial roles in the government. Only the Bolsheviks, the radical wing of the Social Democratic Party, pursued a policy of unconditional opposition to the Provisional Government.

In July 1917, the streets of Petrograd were full of workers protesting the Provisional Government's decision to continue fighting the war. The crisis resulted in the resignation of Lvov and several of his ministers, but the Provisional Government was reconstituted with Kerensky as Prime Minister. In the following months, Kerensky effectively ruled over Russia as a dictator, undermining the Soviet in the process. He appointed General Lavr Kornilov as commander-in-chief and took steps to strengthen the army so that it could more effectively keep order in Petrograd. Within a couple of weeks Kerensky became jealous of Kornilov's growing popularity and became fearful that his commander-in-chief had plans to overthrow the government. The Prime Minister dismissed Kornilov from his post, but this merely encouraged him to order his men to assault the capital. Kerensky mobilized the Petrograd Soviet, including the Bolsheviks, to defend Petrograd from Kornilov. Kerensky's government survived, but the Bolsheviks were the ultimate beneficiaries. They had been suppressed by Kerensky a couple of months earlier but were now feted as the saviors of the revolution. Meanwhile, Kerensky lost the confidence of both the left and right and remained Prime Minister simply because the Soviet refused to overthrow him.

At the end of October, the Bolshevik Party finally decided to stage an armed insurrection to take power. As a result of their opposition to the Provisional Government, the Bolsheviks gained popularity and became the largest political force in Petrograd. Many senior Bolsheviks were reluctant to risk an insurrection, preferring to use the Petrograd Soviet as a vehicle to overthrow the government. Senior Bolsheviks Lev Kamenev and Grigory Zinoviev voted against the insurrection and even warned Kerensky in advance. Nevertheless, Lenin spoke forcefully in favor of an insurrection, which took place on 25 and 26 October. The main coordinator of the operation was Leon Trotsky, Lenin's charismatic second-in-command. The Red Guards under Trotsky's direction seized key strategic positions in Petrograd but failed to achieve their objectives not so much due to any resistance from government forces, but due to confused signals from the leadership. Eventually an assault on the Winter Palace was signaled by a blank round fired by the cruiser *Aurora*. The Red Guards stormed a side staircase, overcoming token opposition, before locating the ministers of the Provisional Government and placing them under arrest early in the morning of 26 October. While the insurrection was still underway, Trotsky proclaimed that the Bolsheviks had taken power in the name of the Soviet. The October Revolution brought Lenin to the pinnacle of power.

Part 3 – Soviet Russia

Chapter 14 – A New Dawn

The October Revolution resulted in the creation of the Council of People's Commissars, the new government led by Lenin as Chairman. The significance of October lay in the fact that power transferred not to a coalition of socialist parties, but a single-party Bolshevik government in Petrograd. A Bolshevik uprising in Moscow was met with greater resistance but eventually prevailed. The Bolsheviks participated in the elections to the Constituent Assembly, but when it became clear that they would not win a majority and would be required to share power, Lenin gave orders for the assembly to be suppressed when it opened in January 1918. After meeting for twenty-four hours, the Constituent Assembly was forcibly closed by Red Guards and the deputies formed an alternative government in the city of Samara on the Volga. The suppression of the Constituent Assembly was a definitive moment when Lenin resolved to rule as a dictator, renaming his party the Russian Communist Party in the process. Although Lenin was persuaded in early 1918 to form a coalition with the Left SRs, the radical wing of the SRs which supported the October Revolution, the coalition fell apart within a couple of months. In August 1918 Lenin was almost killed by an SR terrorist named Fanya Kaplan, who attempted to assassinate Lenin because she believed he had betrayed the revolution. Kaplan was soon executed following interrogation by the Cheka, the secret police Lenin established at the end of 1917 under the leadership of the Polish communist Felix Dzerzhinsky to consolidate Bolshevik power.

As a further step in his consolidation of power, Lenin took steps to end the war with Germany. One of Lenin's first acts was to issue the Decree on Peace, which called for all warring nations to lay down their arms and make peace without any territorial annexations or reparations. The decree was a bold signal, but was not realistic. If Russia were to exit the war, it would have to come to an agreement with Germany. Trotsky, as Foreign Minister, was given the task of negotiating peace. The political turmoil in 1917 caused greater damage to the Russian war effort and the German army was within striking distance of Petrograd, which forced the Bolsheviks to relocate the capital to Moscow. The Germans demanded humiliating terms and Trotsky was hesitant to sign away large parts of territory. Instead, he attempted to stall, expecting that Germany would soon succumb to socialist revolution itself and a peace treaty could be made on friendly terms. By March 1918, the Germans were running out of patience and Lenin gave Trotsky an unconditional order to sign the Treaty of Brest-Litovsk. Lenin recognized that defeat was a humiliation but was aware that it would buy him time to establish Bolshevik power across the country.

The Bolsheviks established the world's first socialist state and attempted to transform Russia according to their radical principles. Almost as soon as he became head of government, Lenin issued the Decree on Land which redistributed land belonging to nobles and transferred them to peasants. The government's commitment to eradicating privilege transformed daily life. The old distinctions of rank were completely eliminated so men and women would simply address each other as "comrade." Russia also looked and sounded different. Instead of the double-headed eagles of the Romanov

Empire, the Bolsheviks adopted red flags and stars, together with the hammer and sickle. Lenin championed avant-garde art, which sought to break through the boundaries of classical art in the same way the Bolsheviks had broken the traditional political system. In terms of music, the solemn hymns of Imperial and Orthodox Russia were replaced by revolutionary songs such as *The Internationale*, the international anthem of workers which called for proletarian solidarity.

As Marxists, the Bolsheviks also attacked religious practices, which Marx famously described as "the opiate of the masses." The Orthodox Church in Russia was an institutional bulwark of conservatism and retained great influence in the countryside. In February Russia adopted the Gregorian Calendar which was in use in western Europe, breaking away from the Julian Calendar which continued to be observed by the Orthodox Church. The Bolsheviks pursued a campaign of religious persecution in an effort to undermine the Church, seizing the property of the Church on behalf of the people. In their pursuit of equality, the Bolsheviks initiated wide-ranging educational reforms. In contrast to the Church which provided only the most basic education to Russian peasants, the Bolsheviks hoped to educate the peasantry in order to encourage the spread of Marxist philosophy. Lenin introduced a reform to Russian orthography by which several letters which could be easily replaced by others were eliminated from the alphabet, thus simplifying the language. Within ten years literacy rates in Russia increased from 40% to 90%. The educational reforms were among the most successful legacies of the revolution.

The radical transformations brought forth by Lenin did not meet with universal approval. Resistance to Bolshevism began almost immediately after the revolution. In the summer of 1918 the Czechoslovak Legion which had served in the Russian army during the war rebelled against the Bolsheviks after being forced to disarm. These experienced soldiers managed to defeat the Bolshevik Red Army in several engagements and occupied much of Siberia. They were approaching Ekaterinburg, where Nicholas II and his family had been imprisoned. Lenin feared that Nicholas would emerge as the rallying point for the White forces – conservative opponents of the Bolshevik regime. Accordingly, Lenin gave orders in July for the former Tsar to be executed together with his family, just a week before the Czechs captured the city. The successes of the Czech Legion enabled Admiral Alexander Kolchak to occupy much of Siberia by 1919. Kolchak captured Samara and displaced the rival socialist government and proclaimed himself Supreme Leader of Russia. In addition to Kolchak, the Bolsheviks were threatened by armies led by General Anton Denikin in the south and by Nikolay Yudenich in the northwest, which threatened to take Petrograd. While all these White armies made significant territorial gains against the Reds, they were eventually beaten back. By 1920 the major threats to the Bolsheviks were eliminated, and in 1921 the remnants of the White movement were evacuated from Crimea to exile in western Europe and the United States.

The survival of the Bolshevik government was far from guaranteed. Many expected Lenin's regime to collapse within a number of weeks. The Bolsheviks initially abolished a permanent army on grounds of principle, but soon realized that it was necessary to maintain an army to confront the counter-revolutionaries. The Red Army was placed under the command of Trotsky, whose organization skills were second to none. Although Kolchak, Denikin and Yudenich had relatively few men under arms, they were highly experienced and supported by small contingents of foreign troops. By contrast, the Red Army was numerous but its soldiers were newly recruited and ill-disciplined. Had the three White armies successfully coordinated their actions, the Reds would have found it much more difficult to resist. Fundamentally, the Red Army won the Civil War due to geographical factors. Although the Bolsheviks occupied less territory than Kolchak, they controlled the main population centers, the majority of industry, and much of the transport infrastructure. This enabled the Red Army to recruit more men and manufacture more weapons. Control of the railroads enabled Red Army divisions to move between fronts and take on the White armies separately. Trotsky forced former tsarist generals into the service of the Red Army by holding their families as hostages. In emergency situations such as the Civil War, officers with aristocratic backgrounds were welcomed by Trotsky in order to train the Red Army. The questionable loyalties of many of these officers would cause problems for the Soviet state a decade later.

Despite victory in the Civil War, Lenin's regime was far from stable by 1921. During the war the Red Army forcibly requisitioned grain from peasants in order to support the war effort. At the same time, they confiscated goods from the Church, ostensibly to buy food for the people. These policies outraged the peasants and alienated them from the government in Moscow. In 1920 and 1921 the Red Army was forced to confront a series of peasant uprisings in the countryside. Lenin believed that this was a far greater threat to the survival of the Bolshevik regime than the White armies. The crisis faced by the Bolsheviks was further underlined by the mutiny of the Kronstadt sailors in March 1921, who protested against the luxuries enjoyed by the political commissars under the Bolshevik government. This event was extremely embarrassing for Lenin. The Kronstadt sailors had been among the most vociferous supporters of the October Revolution and they were celebrated as heroes of the Revolution. The sailors also controlled the Baltic Fleet and could sail their ships to bombard Petrograd once the ice melted. Both of these key issues were addressed by Lenin at the 10th Party Congress in March 1921. He sent a force under Trotsky to suppress the mutinous sailors. The Red Army marched across the ice and bombarded the sailors with artillery, eventually forcing them to surrender. Meanwhile, at the Party Congress Lenin granted concessions to the peasants to pacify the countryside. He introduced a New Economic Policy (NEP) which introduced a limited market for goods. Instead of having their grain requisitioned, the peasants would pay a portion as tax to the state. This was a major retreat from Lenin's economic philosophy, but he understood the need to compromise in order to diffuse opposition.

After coming to power in 1917, Lenin and Bolsheviks struggled with the legacy of the Russian Empire. During the First World War, the Russian empire fragmented and several national entities declared their independence. As Marxists, the Bolsheviks opposed imperialism and believed in national self-determination. Accordingly, they quickly recognized Finnish independence in 1918. However, Lenin also appreciated that the territories of the former empire were rich in resources. The Treaty of Brest-Litovsk was a great humiliation, but the defeat of Germany in 1918 rendered the settlement null and void. During the Civil War the Reds were inclined to defend the territory of the former empire, even if it was not ethnically Russian. In Ukraine, the Reds fought bloody engagements against Nestor Makhno's anarchist Green Army, while in Poland they waged war against Marshal Josef Pilsudski's army. By invading Poland, Lenin and Trotsky hoped to export revolution throughout Europe. The Red Army reached the gates of Warsaw in the spring of 1920 but was beaten back by the summer. Lenin once again conceded defeat and the project to export socialist revolution across Europe was postponed. In 1922, the government established the Union of Soviet Socialist Republics (USSR) as a solution to the nationalities problem. The USSR consisted of twelve member states, including Russia, each of which enjoyed cultural autonomy and some degree of political autonomy, although in reality, the government in Moscow made the key decisions. The creation of the USSR was inspired in large part by Josef Stalin, a Georgian Bolshevik who served as the first People's Commissar for the Nationalities.

Stalin became increasingly influential in Lenin's government after 1922. In early 1922 Lenin appointed Stalin to the post of General Secretary of the Communist Party. The newly-created post controlled appointments to party offices and Lenin saw Stalin as a key supporter of the NEP, which had been vociferously opposed by Trotsky. Lenin had envisaged Stalin as a useful subordinate, but Stalin effectively deputized for Lenin after the party leader suffered a stroke in 1922. He met Lenin regularly at the latter's dacha in

Gorky, serving as the main conduit of information between Lenin and Moscow. Although he appreciated Stalin's support and loyalty, Lenin was critical of Stalin's manner and behavior in certain situations. He was infuriated when he heard that Stalin had insulted his wife, Nadezhda Krupskaya, in a telephone conversation. Lenin sensed that Stalin was becoming too powerful and sought to remove him from his post. He produced a document in the winter of 1922 which became known as his Testament, where he proposed changes to the structure of the government. He assessed the qualities of six leading party figures and concluded that if any single individual were to succeed him, the party would be split, with potentially serious consequences for the survival of the Soviet state. Lenin's Testament described Stalin as "coarse" and unfit for the post of General Secretary and recommended that he be replaced by an individual who would share all of Stalin's qualities but would be "more polite and considerate to comrades." Lenin hoped that his testament could be presented to the 12th Party Congress meeting in the spring of 1923, but suffered a third stroke which left him unable to speak. Krupskaya kept the testament secret in the hope that Lenin would recover his facilities, but he died in January 1924. The bold visionary who led the October Revolution was dead. The party and the country had to decide how best to achieve Lenin's vision.

Chapter 15 – Terror and Upheaval

Lenin's death provoked an outpouring of grief across the country and in the Bolshevik party. The party leaders eulogized Lenin and hailed him for his visionary leadership. The city of Petrograd was renamed Leningrad in his honor. Against the wishes of his widow, the state decided to preserve Lenin's body in a mausoleum on Red Square. Despite Lenin's call for collective leadership after his demise, a struggle for power soon ensued between the members of the Politburo – the supreme decision-making body of the Communist Party. The highest profile Politburo member was Trotsky, whose contribution to the Revolution and the Civil War cannot be underestimated. However, Trotsky's popularity was a source of jealousy among his fellow leaders, who resented Trotsky for assuming a prominent leadership role despite aligning himself formally to the Bolsheviks as late as the summer of 1917. Stalin, Kamenev, and Zinoviev formed a political alliance to sideline Trotsky. The latter had been opposed to the NEP and therefore enjoyed less authority in the government. Trotsky was recuperating from illness in the Caucasus when he heard of Lenin's death and was absent from Lenin's funeral, while Stalin organized the event and served as one of the pallbearers. Lenin's Testament was made public, but Kamenev and Zinoviev protected Stalin while Trotsky stayed quiet. By 1925, Trotsky was effectively consigned to the political wilderness.

At the same time, Stalin began to advocate for a policy of "Socialism in one country," arguing that the Soviet state should work to establish communism within the Soviet Union before attempting to encourage global revolution. This placed him at odds with Trotsky, but the policy was also challenged by Kamenev and Zinoviev. By 1926 the political alliances began to shift as Stalin moved towards the right of the party, siding with Nikolay Bukharin and Alexey Rykov, both of whom were enthusiastic supporters of the NEP. Kamenev and Zinoviev regarded the NEP as a temporary concession to pragmatism but believed that the state should eventually impose direct control over economic life in the countryside, and now that the countryside was pacified the Bolsheviks should once again impose state control. They formed a United Opposition with Trotsky against the Rightists, but Stalin and Bukharin managed to defeat them in party debates. Although they counted on support from old Bolsheviks, Kamenev and Zinoviev were encumbered by the fact they had voted against the insurrection in October 1917, and the Rightists managed to force them out of the Politburo by labeling them anti-Leninists. In the process, Stalin promoted several allies into the Politburo, including Lazar Kaganovich, Kliment Voroshilov, and Vyacheslav Molotov.

In 1928, Stalin abruptly abandoned his support for the NEP and proposed radical economic reforms which amounted to state control of economic life. In October he announced the first Five Year Plan which entailed the collectivization of agriculture, together with rapid industrialization, setting ambitious targets for industrial production. Stalin's sudden shift in policy took Bukharin by surprise. Bukharin defended the NEP and believed collectivization would destabilize the countryside. Once again, Stalin mobilized his loyal supporters in the party and expelled his erstwhile ally from the Politburo in 1929. According to official figures, the first Five Year Plan was a great success. Industrial output grew by at least 15 percent and at the end 1932 Stalin announced that the production targets had been met – nine months in advance. Industrialization transformed the Soviet economy. Industrial centers appeared in the middle of the Siberian wilderness. The population of the remote settlement of Magnitogorsk increased to a quarter of the million after the construction of steelworks which would make the city the main center of iron and steel output for the country.

Collectivization transformed the Russian agrarian economy beyond recognition. For centuries Russian peasants farmed individual strips of land. Under serfdom, the surplus produce was transferred to landowners, but under the NEP peasants could buy and sell any surpluses in local markets. Wealthier peasants, known as kulaks, would use the profits generated from these sales to buy land from their neighbors and consolidate their holdings. This made it economically viable to use agricultural machinery to cultivate the land. Stalin sought to end the practice of strip farming but was also opposed to the kulaks making profits at the expense of fellow farmers. The process of collectivization would create collective farms across the country. The peasants would work together to farm the land more efficiently and transfer a quota of their produce to the state. Initially collectivization was designed to be a voluntary process, but peasants throughout the country were so overwhelmingly opposed to collectivization that party officials usually had to coerce peasants into collectivization. By the end of the First Year Plan more than two-thirds of agricultural land in the Soviet Union was collectivized. Although state control of agriculture enabled the government to allocate produce to the factory workers in newly industrialized centers, the quotas could not be fulfilled during times of poor harvest, resulting in widespread famine. In 1932-33 famine swept across country, claiming the lives of several million Ukrainian farmers alone. This has been referred to as a policy of state genocide, but famine affected the entirety of the USSR and the state was in no position to provide sufficient food for the whole country.

The horrors of collectivization were only one aspect of an increasingly brutal regime under Stalin. By 1930 the General Secretary had maneuvered between his political rivals to become the undisputed leader of the Soviet Union, and in the process he made many enemies. In the mid-1930s he pursued a campaign of terror to eliminate any potential threat to his rule. The terror began in 1934 following the assassination of Sergey Kirov, the popular head of the Communist Party in Leningrad. Kirov was Stalin's ally but Stalin seems to have regarded him as a potential challenger to his authority. Kirov's assassination in December 1934 may have been carried out on the orders of Stalin, but the evidence remains unclear. In any case, over the next four years Stalin ordered the NKVD (the organization which succeeded the Cheka) to arrest hundreds and thousands of party members, charging them with treason and complicity in Kirov's assassination. Among the high-profile victims of the purge were Lev Kamenev and Grigory Zinoviev, who were subjected to show trials in Moscow in 1936 which condemned them to execution. Two years later, Bukharin and Rykov were subjected to the same procedure. Bukharin denied the spurious charges against him for three months, but finally confessed after threats against his family and executed in March 1938. Among the members of Lenin's Politburo only Trotsky seemed out of reach in exile in Mexico, but in 1940 he was assassinated by a Mexican agent under Stalin's orders. The terror was pervasive and affected every level of social life. Children were encouraged to inform on their parents. Those who escaped the firing squad would be sent to gulags (labor camps) in Siberia. Many innocent individuals were condemned, and two heads of the NKVD – Genrikh Yagoda and Nikolay Yezhov, were themselves executed during the purge for their "mistakes."

The scope of Stalin's Great Terror extended beyond the Communist Party. During the Great Terror senior army officers were suspected of disloyalty and fell victim to the purges. Stalin had good reason to be suspicious of the political loyalty of the Red Army. The army was founded by Trotsky and many commanders retained their admiration of his leadership. Furthermore, many officers had aristocratic backgrounds and there was a risk that in the event of war with capitalist enemies, these men would conspire with the enemy to overthrow communism. The highest profile army officer to fall victim to the purge was Mikhail Tukhachevsky, an intelligent military commander and theoretician who was the most talented officer in the Soviet army. Throughout the 1920s and 1930s Tukhachevsky was responsible for the modernization of the Soviet army's tactics and strategy in an era of mechanized warfare. Stalin begrudgingly recognized Tukhachevsky's talents and contributions and appointed him Marshal of the Soviet Union, the highest rank in the Soviet Army established in 1935. Tukhachevsky was a popular commander in the army and Stalin was anxious that he would launch a military coup, following the example of Napoleon Bonaparte who overthrew the French Revolutionary government. In 1937 Tukhachevsky was accused of plotting with Bukharin to overthrow the government and executed. His fellow Marshals Vasily Blyukher and Alexander Yegorov would also face the firing squad in 1938 and 1939 respectively.

Stalin's purge of the army was carried out in a period of increasing political tensions both in Europe and Asia. In 1933 Adolf Hitler was appointed Chancellor of Germany and assumed the post of President and Fuhrer the following year. Hitler's National Socialist (Nazi) Party was ideologically opposed to communism and regarded the Slavic peoples as racially inferior. The central theme of Hitler's ideology was the eastward expansion of Germany towards Poland, Lithuania, and Belarus, displacing the Slavic and Jewish populations to create *Lebensraum* – living space to provide for the prosperity of the German people. Consequently, Germany and the USSR could be expected to be at war with each other sooner rather than later. Stalin sought an alliance with France and the United Kingdom directed against the threat of Nazi Germany. In 1934 the USSR had joined the League of Nations, the international body created by the victors of the First World War to maintain the post-war international order. During this time the French and British were reluctant to confront Hitler and pursued a policy of appeasement and Stalin's diplomatic overtures were rejected while the British and French governments allowed Hitler to annex Austria and occupy Czechoslovakia in 1938 and 1939.

By 1939, Stalin's hopes of negotiating an anti-Hitler alliance were ebbing away, leading to a change in Soviet foreign policy. He dismissed his Foreign Minister Maxim Litvinov and appointed his loyal subordinate Vyacheslav Molotov in his place. Stalin instructed Molotov to open diplomatic channels with German Foreign Minister Joachim Ribbentrop in an effort to receive guarantees from Hitler that Germany would not take up arms against the USSR. The change of personnel allowed Stalin greater control over negotiations since Litvinov had openly advocated for an anti-Hitler alliance, while Molotov was prepared to carry out Stalin's orders. Molotov continued negotiations with Britain and France, but failed to come to an agreement after talks in August. The British and French were concerned about the prospect of the Red Army operating in Poland, and believed that the Soviets would not be faithful allies, while the Soviets were disappointed by the numbers of troops the British and French were willing to contribute to the cause. Molotov adjourned the talks with Britain and France and instead came to an understanding with Germany, which was finalized on 24 August 1939. Under the terms of the Molotov-Ribbentrop Non-Aggression Pact, Germany and the USSR committed to avoid war against each other for ten years. The agreement included secret clauses in which Poland would be divided between Germany and the USSR. News of the Nazi-Soviet rapprochement shocked European political observers, who were unaware that the two powers were engaged in secret negotiations. On 1 September, Hitler invaded Poland, provoking Britain and France into declaring war against Germany and marking the beginning of the Second World War. Two weeks later Soviet armies joined the invasion, and by the end of the month Polish territory was entirely occupied. Once Poland had been erased from the map by German and Russian armies.

The secret protocols of the Molotov-Ribbentrop Pact also provided for the Soviet annexation of the Baltic states of Estonia, Latvia, and Lithuania, which had broken away from the Russian Empire during the aftermath of the First World War and the 1917 revolutions. At the end of November 1939, the Red Army invaded Finland ostensibly for purposes of security, since Leningrad was a mere twenty miles from the Finnish border. The Soviets and the Finnish army fought for three months in a bloody war during the winter of 1939-40. The Finns defended resolutely behind the Mannerheim Line, a series of defensive positions constructed under the supervision of Field Marshal Carl Gustaf Mannerheim, formerly an officer in the Russian Imperial Army. When the peace was signed in March 1940, the Soviets made some modest territorial gains but sustained substantial losses. Estimates suggest that the Soviets lost around half of their 700,000 men and a considerable amount of machinery. The Finnish army was half the size but only suffered 20 percent casualties. The lackluster performance of the Red Army, weakened by Stalin's purges, informed Hitler that the Soviet Union was not an effective military force.

Chapter 16 – The Great Patriotic War

On 22 June 1941, 3 million German soldiers along an 1800-mile front crossed the border into the USSR and launched Operation Barbarossa, the codename for the German invasion of the Soviet Union. The operation was named after Frederick Barbarossa, a medieval German Emperor who ruled over much of Europe. Despite receiving advance warning from Soviet intelligence officers that the Nazis were preparing a large-scale offensive against the USSR, Stalin doubted their credibility and was surprised by the invasion. He forbade the Soviet army from returning fire. Once he realized the invasion was genuine, he sank into a deep depression, leaving the army retreating in disorder. German tanks advanced 200 miles in a week. When a group of political and military leaders met him at his dacha requesting orders, Stalin believed they had come to arrest him. Once he was persuaded that he was still in charge, Stalin ordered the army not to retreat a single step and decreed that anyone seen retreating would be shot. These orders worsened the strategic situation, forcing isolated Soviet units to fight to the death instead of allowing them to regroup to launch a counterattack.

Like Napoleon's Grande Armée before him, Hitler's Wehrmacht (the German Army) launched a three-pronged attack aimed at Leningrad, Moscow, and southern Russia via Ukraine respectively. Unlike Napoleon, Hitler designated an equal weight to all three fronts and aimed to strike simultaneously in three directions. Early in September 1941, the German armies were approaching Leningrad from the west and south, their Finnish allies by the north. The siege itself started in September, with all supply lines, railways and highways cut by the Germans on 30 August. The authorities had no time to evacuate civilians but some priceless artistic treasures from the Hermitage Museum were evacuated. Soviet counterattacks to lift the siege were unsuccessful and the siege would last almost 900 days. Leningrad was subjected large-scale air raids by the Luftwaffe (German air force), but the more dangerous threat to the lives of Leningraders was the constant bombardment of artillery shells. The city suffered from terrible food shortages. Only a small amount of the supplies could go through the blockade from across Lake Ladoga. The supply route would soon be known as the Road of Life. Despite the effort, starvation, diseases and shelling would cause the deaths of 650,000 Leningraders in 1942 alone. The composer Dmitry Shostakovich's Seventh Symphony vividly portrayed the siege and became a symbol of Leningrad's defiance against the invaders. The Soviet armies were determined to save Leningrad. It was a city of great significance, not only a former capital but a large industrial center and the base of the Baltic Fleet. Early in 1943, the Soviet offensives broke through the encirclement, which allowed more supplies to reach the shores of Lake Ladoga. But the siege was not lifted until January 1944 after a successful Soviet counter-offensive. As they retreated, the Nazis blew up important cultural landmarks including the imperial palaces at Tsarskoe Selo and Peterhof.

The German units sent towards Moscow traversed the same path as the Grande Armée more than a century earlier. In October 1941 Germans and Soviets clashed at Borodino, the site of the great battle in 1812. The Germans seized control of the battlefield and continued their advance towards Moscow. In anticipation, Lenin's body was evacuated to Kuibyshev (Samara), and the government made plans for evacuation but Stalin decided to stay put at the last minute. The task of defending Moscow fell to General Georgy Zhukov, commander of the Western Front. The advance of the German armies began to slow down with the onset of winter, but the Soviet Army was required to rapidly replenish its ranks following the devastating losses earlier in the summer. On 7 November 1941, Stalin held the traditional military parade in Red Square in honor of the October Revolution. 100,000 men of the Reserve Army marched past the Kremlin and to the strains of patriotic marches straight towards the front lines. Although the Soviet defensive positions were precarious, the Wehrmacht was encumbered by mud and ice and unable to operate effectively. The Soviet troops suffered the same privations but were better equipped for the cold weather. The German command ordered to halt the offensive in early December. Zhukov subsequently launched a counter-offensive which pushed the Wehrmacht back 200 miles, relieving Moscow from immediate danger.

In the summer of 1942, Hitler turned his attention south. His armies already occupied Ukraine and was pushing east. The ultimate strategic objective was to seize the oil fields in the Caucasus which fueled the Soviet war machine. The initial target was the city of Stalingrad, which was not only an important industrial center but located strategically on the lower reaches of the River Volga. The Wehrmacht began its assault on Stalingrad on 23 August 1942. Heavy bombardment both from the air reduced much of the city to rubble, but the Soviets defended resolutely when the German 6th Army advanced into Stalingrad. The Germans were expecting to gain control of the city in short order but underestimated the tenacity of the Soviet defenders. Over the course of three months the armies engaged in fierce hand-to-hand fighting. One of the iconic symbols of Soviet resistance was Pavlov's House, an apartment building which managed to resist capture by the German forces for two months before it was relieved. The city bearing Stalin's name had great symbolic importance for both armies and encapsulated the brutality of the war. The city had been named after Stalin in 1925 in recognition of his leadership during the Battle of Tsaritsyn in 1920 during the Civil War. The Soviet Army could not envisage relinquishing control of Stalingrad to the Nazis.

In November the Germans reached the Volga, but the fierce fighting in Stalingrad had taken its toll. Zhukov devised an ambitious plan to attack the Hungarian and Romanian armies which were protecting the flanks of the German 6th Army. On 19 November the Soviets launched Operation Uranus, sending two groups against the northern and southern flanks of the invading army. The Soviets made rapid progress against the weaker Hungarians and Romanians and on 23 November successfully surrounded the 6th Army. Their commander, General Friedrich von Paulus, requested permission to break out and abandon the city, but Hitler gave orders to stand firm. The Soviets slowly encroached and closed the ring while the Germans were without food in the middle of winter. In February Hitler promoted Paulus to Field Marshal. Since no German Field Marshal had been captured by the enemy, Paulus was expected to fight to the death or commit suicide. He confounded Hitler's expectations and surrendered. He remained in Soviet captivity for the rest of the war, producing anti-Hitler propaganda and serving as an informal military advisor to the Soviet command.

The Battle of Stalingrad, which involved over 2 million men from both sides, was the largest battle in world history. It was also the turning point in the Eastern Front. The Wehrmacht were on the retreat and the initiative passed to the Soviet Army under Zhukov's command. The German military strategy had comprehensively failed. In July 1943 Hitler attempted to regain the initiative by ordering an offensive at Kursk. The offensive was well-signaled and both sides rushed reinforcements into the front. After a brief Soviet bombardment, the Germans began the offensive with artillery shelling, then infantry, supported by the Luftwaffe. The battle would become the greatest tank battle in history. The Wehrmacht hoped that their tanks would overwhelm the Soviets and move rapidly into enemy territory, but they were held back by the Soviets fighting obstinately from their defensive positions. Five days later, the advance from the north was stopped. In the south, the German accomplished a little more. On 12 July, the Soviets launched the counteroffensive Operation Kutuzov and drove the Germans to their positions before the offensive twelve days later. By the end of the battle, the Soviet Army suffered greater casualties, but the Germans lost their momentum and would never regain the strategic initiative.

After its defeat at Kursk, the Wehrmacht was a shadow of its former self. By the summer of 1944, they found it increasingly difficult to replenish men and vehicles on the Eastern Front. To make matters worse, British and American forces landed in Normandy on D-Day, thus pushing the Germans onto a two-front war. Stalin had long requested the opening for a second front in the west from US President Franklin D. Roosevelt and British Prime Minister Winston Churchill. The Soviets launched an offensive to recapture Belarus shortly after D-Day. The operation was codenamed Bagration after the hero of the Napoleonic invasion. Operation Bagration was one of the best-planned strategic operations in history. On 19 June, the Wehrmacht faced an attack from the Red Army partisans from behind their lines, followed by massive air attacks two days later. On 23 June, Soviet armies moved forward and caught the Germans by surprise. Seeing that the German were ordered to stand firm, the Soviet pushed forward and left German units isolated in scattered pockets in hostile territory. The victory of the Red Army was remarkable. In early July, they retook the Belorussian capital of Minsk.

Operation Bagration took the Soviet Army into Eastern Poland. Although they were fighting on the same side, relations between the Polish resistance and the Soviet military were poor, since the Soviets had earlier invaded Poland under the Molotov-Ribbentrop Pact. In 1940, the NKVD executed 6,000 Polish officers at Katyn and buried them in a mass grave. Although Stalin denied perpetrating the crime, the Polish government-in-exile in London suspected it had been carried out by the Soviets. These tensions encouraged the Polish Home Army to attempt to oust the Germans from Warsaw before the Soviets could. The revolt started on 1 August when the Warsaw corps, 50,000 men strong, attacked the German authorities. They gained control of Warsaw, but the Germans sent in reinforcements and bombarded the city for the next two months. The Red Army was across the other side of the Vistula at Praga, but refused to provide any assistance to the Polish rebels. Moreover, they refused to let the other Allies use their air bases for airlifting supplies to the Poles. In October, the Home Army was scattered and forced to surrender when their supplies ran out. The Nazis flattened the city and deported Warsaw's civilian population. The Home Army was obliterated. This played into Stalin's hands. There would be fewer obstacles when the Soviets occupied all of Poland and installed a communist government.

The Red Army went through Poland to the River Oder, where they accumulated their fighting force in preparation for an assault on Berlin in the spring of 1945. The western Allies were only 60 miles away. There was little hope left for the Germans. Nonetheless, Berlin was putting up its last resistance. The Nazi Party recruited all men from 16 to 60 years old into the Volkssturm, their equivalent of the Home Guard. Inside Berlin, life went on. Shops were still opened, factories were still working. But there was an obvious air of fear and pressure and Nazi devotees were executing everyone they thought to be traitors and deserters. Artillery shells were fired into Berlin for three weeks and the 1,000,000-men strong infantry assault followed. The advance went slowly, street by street. But Berlin did not withstand for long. Stalin hoped to beat his Allies to Berlin, and sent his generals, Zhukov and Konev, to race to Berlin, which resulted in heavy casualties. Nevertheless, Stalin achieved his geopolitical goal. Hitler committed suicide on 30 April and on 1 May the Soviet flag flew above the Reichstag building. The German surrender was signed in the presence of British, American, and Soviet representatives late on the evening of 8 May. Due to the time difference, it was already 9 May in Moscow, and thus 9 May was designated Victory Day in the Soviet Union.

Victory over Germany marked the end of the Great Patriotic War, the USSR's struggle for survival against Nazism, but the Second World War was not over. At the Potsdam Conference in July 1945, the three leaders of the Allied powers – Harry S. Truman, Winston Churchill and Josef Stalin – met to discuss the future of Europe and the war against Japan. Stalin agreed with the western Allies that he would join the war against Japan. At Potsdam, President Truman informed Stalin about "a new weapon" which had recently been developed in the United States. The atomic bombing of Hiroshima and Nagasaki on 6 and 9 August, together with the Soviet invasion on 9 August, were motivating factors in Japan's unconditional surrender to the Allies. Within a couple of weeks, Soviet forces swept captured Manchuria and the northern half of the Korean Peninsula, while American forces secured control of the southern half. The disposition of Soviet and Allied forces in Europe and Asia at the end of the Second World War would have far-reaching consequences for the rest of the twentieth century and beyond.

Chapter 17 – Cold War

The Allied victory in the Second World War saw Soviet and American troops exchange fraternal greetings, respecting each other for the hardships they had endured during the brutal war. Nevertheless, there remained significant ideological and geopolitical differences between the Soviet Union and their western allies – the US, Britain, and France. The Soviet Union had suffered greatly from the Nazi invasion, which cost 27 million Soviet lives. Stalin demanded territorial compensation, but the expansion of the Soviet state and its influence proved a concern to the western powers. The Americans and British proposed to rebuild the German industry to restore economic activity and facilitate the rebuilding of Europe, but the Soviets resisted the prospect of a resurgent Germany. As a result of their differences, the Allies divided Germany and Berlin into four zones of occupation. By 1948, the three western zones were consolidated into the Federal Republic of Germany (West Germany), while the Soviet zone became the German Democratic Republic (East Germany). The division of Germany between western and Soviet influence was mirrored in Europe. Already in 1946, Winston

Churchill remarked in a speech at Fulton, Missouri, "from Stettin in the Baltic to Trieste in the Adriatic an iron curtain has descended across the Continent." The iron curtain came to describe the divide between the capitalist states of western Europe and communist Eastern Europe. The United States and the Soviet Union were thus engaged in the Cold War – an ideological and geopolitical struggle fought through regional proxies.

Tensions between Stalin and his erstwhile allies were also apparent in Asia. China had been engaged in a civil war between the Nationalist government of Chiang Kai-Shek and the Communist insurgency under Mao Zedong. The two warring parties cooperated to resist Japanese invasion during WWII but came into conflict once again. The United States supported the Nationalist government, and although Stalin did not openly support Mao, the Soviets provided the Red Army with a well-equipped base in Manchuria. By 1949, the Communists secured victory and forced the Nationalist government into exile in Taiwan. The Americans and Soviets also came into conflict over the future of the Korean peninsula, which was divided between a communist government in the north and a pro-western one in the south. The North Korean leader Kim Il-Sung hoped to launch an invasion of the south to reunify Korea under a communist government, but Stalin was reluctant to support the venture. He eventually sanctioned the invasion in 1950, but envisaged that Mao's China would assist Kim if required. In 1950-53, the North Korean army supported by primarily Chinese forces and Soviet advisors struggled desperately against the South Korean army and their American allies. The momentum swung back and forth between the opposing forces, but both sides were eventually deadlocked and agreed to peace along the 38th parallel, the effective border before the war.

Stalin's health began to decline in the 1950s. In 1952, Stalin was informed by his doctor that his health was only getting worse and that it would be in his best interests to take things easy. The General Secretary was angry at this suggestion and ordered that the doctor be arrested. Fueled by paranoia, Stalin believed there was a Doctor's Plot to assassinate Soviet leaders and ordered many of Russia's leading physicians to be dismissed and arrested. On 1 March 1953, Stalin was found semi-conscious in his dacha after suffering a cerebral hemorrhage. When the members Politburo arrived at the dacha, they could not decide what to do and hesitated to send for a doctor due to Stalin's suspicions about doctors. By the time a doctor arrived, it was clear that Stalin would not survive. The Politburo leaders began plotting among themselves for the succession by Stalin's bedside. Stalin briefly regained his senses and sat up from his bed, leaving the audience horrified and afraid of reprisals. He soon fell unconscious once again and died on 5 March.

Stalin's death triggered a struggle for succession among the Politburo. He had eliminated all his political opponents and the survivors had all been his protégés. Having reached the summit of the Soviet political system through their loyalty to Stalin, they could not conceive of political life without him. The Politburo agreed that no single individual should assume the leadership and therefore separated Stalin's titles. Georgy Malenkov became Premier and head of government, while Nikita Khrushchev became First Secretary (rather than General Secretary) of the Communist Party. This system of collective leadership would not last long. The first person to challenge for power was Lavrenty Beria, the Georgian head of the NKVD. After Stalin's death he assumed the position of Deputy Premier to the ineffectual Malenkov. As head of the notorious secret service, Beria was viewed with suspicion and fear by the rest of the leadership. In a surprising move, Beria hoped to improve relations with the United States so that the USSR could receive financial aid to rebuild its economy after the devastation of the Second World War. He was prepared to abandon the ideological struggle of the Cold War, and even allow the reunification of Germany. This position brought him into conflict with his Politburo colleagues, who believed it would undermine Soviet power. In June 1953 Khrushchev persuaded the party leadership to stage a coup against Beria, to which Malenkov reluctantly acquiesced. Beria was duly arrested by a group of armed officers under Zhukov's command and executed for treason in December.

Malenkov and Khrushchev shared power for two years following Beria's removal, but the former was dismissed as Premier in 1955 due to his previous association with Beria and succeeded by Nikolay Bulganin. Malenkov's dismissal signaled Khrushchev's ascendancy, although he would not assume the office of Premier until 1958. Although Khrushchev had been a loyal Stalinist, during his leadership of the party he gradually abandoned Stalin's legacy. In February 1956, he delivered a "Secret Speech" to a closed session of the 20th Party Congress attacking Stalin's legacy. In a four-hour address, Khrushchev criticized Stalin's dictatorship, arrests, deportations and his leadership during the war. The speech was a revelation to party members who had been accustomed to praising Stalin. Khrushchev attacked Stalin's cult of personality and initiated a policy of de-Stalinization. In 1961, Stalingrad was renamed Volgograd, and Stalin's embalmed body was removed from Lenin's Mausoleum and buried in the ground behind the mausoleum.

The Khrushchev era would be noted for relaxation of political control – many political prisoners were released, and artistic censorship was relaxed. He pursued reforms to the Soviet economy and the Communist Party. Khrushchev was concerned about food production and promoted the cultivation of corn in Ukraine and the Virgin Lands. The First Secretary's enthusiasm for corn resulted in the crop being planted in unsuitable lands and the policy was a failure. In urban areas, Khrushchev ordered the construction of apartment blocks to provide accommodation to the Soviet people. Although the Khrushchev apartments were considered poor quality and a blight on Moscow's skyline, they provided affordable housing for Muscovites and were popular at the time.

Khrushchev achieved some notable successes in the Cold War, especially in regard to space exploration. The satellite Sputnik was launched in 1957, a Soviet rocket arrived in the moon in 1959 and Yuri Gagarin became the first man in space in 1961. Gagarin became an instant celebrity and was feted around the world, including the west. Khrushchev's rule is usually associated with a thaw which eased some of the tensions of the Cold War. He aimed for peaceful co-existence with the west and invited US Vice President Richard Nixon to visit Moscow in July 1959, making a return visit to the United States in September, thus becoming the first Soviet leader to visit the United States. Despite this ideal of "peaceful co-existence", the Khrushchev period did result in episodes of confrontation. In 1961 he approved the construction of the Berlin Wall to separate East and West Berlin in an effort to stop people from escaping to the west from the east. In 1962, Cold War tensions reached their height when the Soviet Union sent nuclear missiles to Cuba, which had fallen to a Communist revolution in 1959. US President John F. Kennedy ordered a blockade of Soviet vessels heading into Cuba and forced Khrushchev to the negotiating table. Khrushchev agreed to move the weapons, while Kennedy agreed to take American nuclear weapons back from Turkey. Eventually, a partial ban on nuclear tests would be signed between the Soviet Union, the United States and the United Kingdom in July 1963.

Khrushchev's reforms to the economy and the party apparatus were not universally popular among the party. There was a sense that after denouncing Stalin's cult of personality, Khrushchev was in the process of creating his own. Although Khrushchev did not terrorize the party like Stalin, he frequently promoted and demoted personnel and caused a sense of unease among party officials. In 1964 Khrushchev was removed in a coup led by Leonid Ilyich Brezhnev. Brezhnev had been a supporter of Khrushchev in the struggle against Malenkov and was elevated to the Politburo in 1957. However, as an old-school communist, Brezhnev was a critic of Khrushchev's split with China in the 1960s, and his decision to back down during the Cuban Missile Crisis. When he took power, he restored the title of General Secretary of the Communist Party and ended Khrushchev's reforms. The ousted Khrushchev was forced into retirement and died in 1971.

The Brezhnev period ushered in an era of stability. The Stalinist terror was in the past, as were Khrushchev's ambitious but misguided reforms. An active civil society developed in cities such as Moscow and Leningrad. Soviet citizens enjoyed sporting activities and holiday in the Crimea. For many Soviet people, Brezhnev's rule represented a Golden Era for the Soviet Union. Yet another aspect of the stability under Brezhnev was economic stagnation. By the 1970s, economic growth slowed to 1-2% a year. Soviet state enterprises failed to effectively introduce new technologies to industrial processes. The economic slowdown led to increased black-market activities. Criminals bribed bureaucrats in their efforts to seek profit in this era of stagnation. Corruption scandals were common among party elites. Brezhnev's Politburo had access to luxury items imported from the United States which were restricted to state officials, while most of the population were limited to low-quality domestic products. Living standards continued to fall and by the 1980s the USSR was importing food from the USA more than ever. Earnings from energy export largely went to funding the military industry, especially after the Soviet invasion of Afghanistan in 1980.

Economic stagnation was accompanied by political stagnation. Brezhnev's unwillingness to remove party officials from their posts resulted in gerontocracy – government by the old. By the mid-1970s Brezhnev was a sickly man and incapable of exercising power effectively. The average age of the Politburo was over 70. Although many Soviet leaders recognized the political and economic problems facing the USSR, they were either incapable or unwilling to conceiving bold new ideas to address these issues. The policies of the ruling elite at the time were often compared with Stalin's policies. They were relied on central planning rather than market forces to determine prices. Although state propaganda continued to claim successes of communism, a growing chorus of cynicism emerged in the background. Political dissidents produced literature critical of the regime and circulated it in hand-copied form – a process known as *samizdat*. Brezhnev sought to censor this seditious literature and suppress political dissent.

The Brezhnev period saw a general escalation of the Cold War throughout the world. Over the course of the 1960s and 1970s American armed forces were engaged in battle against communist North Vietnam. Soviet and Chinese special advisors assisted the North Vietnamese which fought stubbornly against US forces and eventually secured victory in 1975. Meanwhile, the Soviets were actively trying to expand its influence in the Middle East, supporting the Arab states in Six Day War against US-backed Israel in 1967. The Soviets consolidated their grip on Eastern Europe in 1968, launching an invasion of Czechoslovakia to suppress the Prague Spring – a series of demonstrations in the Czech capital in support of Alexander Dubcek's reformist government. Struggles in Angola following independence from Portugal in 1975 constituted another element of the Cold War, and in 1980 Soviet troops invaded Afghanistan.

Despite these escalations, Cold War tensions were easing by the end of Brezhnev's rule as both the USSR and the USA adopted a policy of *détente*. US President Richard Nixon sought to end American involvement in Vietnam and initiate warmer diplomatic relations with both China and the USSR. In May 1972, Nixon visited Moscow to hold discussions with Brezhnev. The United States and the Soviet Union signed agreements to co-operate in protecting the environment and in space exploration. Nixon and Brezhnev signed the first Strategic Arms Limitation Treaty (SALT), where both sides agreed to limit their nuclear arms and committed to denuclearization in the future. The height of the détente process came in 1975 with the Conference on Security and Co-operation in Europe in Helsinki. Representatives from 35 nations, including the Soviet Union and the United States, signed the Helsinki Accords, which recognized the sovereignty and territorial integrity of participating states, as well as providing for human rights and national self-determination. The conference was a major diplomatic triumph for Brezhnev as it recognized the Soviet hegemony of eastern Europe, while the United States welcomed Soviet commitments to protecting human rights. Although the United States and the Soviet Union continued to clash on ideological grounds, the Helsinki Accords conveyed the sense that both the United States and the Soviet Union would continue to exist as sovereign states for a long time and the two sides had to establish dialogue to resolve their differences in the interests of global security.

Chapter 18 – Reform and Collapse

Brezhnev's health declined in the late 1970s and he died in November 1982. His immediate successor was Yury Andropov, a former head of the KGB who had only been promoted to the Politburo in May. As head of the KGB, Andropov had a reputation for pursuing harsh, repressive policies, but he promoted younger reform-minded politicians in the party hierarchy. Andropov soon suffered from serious ill-health himself and died in February 1984. Although Andropov indicated his preference for the 52-year-old Mikhail Gorbachev as his successor, his rival Konstantin Chernenko was elected General Secretary by the aging Politburo with Gorbachev as his deputy. Chernenko was already mortally ill and Gorbachev often deputized for the General Secretary in Politburo meetings. By Chernenko's death in March 1985, Gorbachev was widely assumed to be the natural successor and was duly unanimously elected General Secretary by the Politburo.

Mikhail Sergeyevich Gorbachev was born to Russian-Ukrainian peasants in Stavropol in southwestern Russia in 1931. He lived through the famine of 1932-1933 and both of his grandfathers were arrested on false charges. During the Second World War his native village fell under Nazi occupation. He received news that his father had been killed in action, before the family was informed that it was a case of mistaken identity. Gorbachev had high ambitions and entered the law school of Moscow State University in 1952. While at university, he joined the Communist Party and met Raisa Titarenko, whom he married in 1953. Although Gorbachev could have found positions in Moscow, he decided to move back to Stavropol with his wife. Thanks to the patronage of leading party ideologue Mikhail Suslov, Gorbachev rose up the hierarchy in the local Komsomol (Young Communists League) and the party organs in Stavropol. He became a member of the Central Committee of the Communist Party in 1971 and Secretary of Agriculture in 1978, succeeding Fyodor Kulakov, another political patron. In 1980, he became a full member of the Politburo at the age of 49. By the time he was elected General Secretary in 1985, he remained the youngest member of the Politburo.

When he became General Secretary, Gorbachev appointed reform-minded allies to his government including Nikolay Ryzhkov, who managed economic affairs, and Yegor Ligachev, who was placed in charge of personnel. Gorbachev introduced an ambitious reform program to address the economic stagnation of the Brezhnev era. In a speech in Leningrad in May 1985, Gorbachev openly criticized the economic system and emphasized the need to reform. He made frequent visits to farms and factories across the country in order to talk to farmers and factory owners about their difficulties. In February 1986, Gorbachev gave a speech at the 27th Party Congress about the need for restructuring of political and economic system, transparency and openness. Gorbachev's economic reforms are encapsulated by the term *perestroika*. Perestroika (restructuring) started with the loosening of the state control on businesses, allowing farmers and manufacturers to choose their own products, quantity and pricing. This provided economic actors with incentives to make profits and increase production. Moreover, a new policy was introduced to allow limited co-operative businesses, leading to new private businesses. The state allowed for limited free-market capitalism which had not been seen in the USSR since the times of the NEP. Restrictions on foreign trade were also loosened as the bureaucratic system was restructured. Initially, Gorbachev also encouraged western investment, but later backed down and called for the businesses to be Russian-owned.

Gorbachev's economic reforms were accompanied by political reforms. In his speech at the 27th Party Congress, he called for "a new era of transparency and openness." Gorbachev's program of political reforms was introduced under the slogan of *glasnost* (openness). The slogan itself would mean more open and transparent in government activities. The media had previously been under the state's control and every publication was subjected to censorship. Criticism of party officials, whether at the village level or the Union-level, was shut down. Gorbachev saw glasnost as a means to replace the lower levels of the Soviet bureaucracy with a younger generation of reform-minded officials who would implement Gorbachev's economic reforms at the local level. But the policy soon brought light upon the harsh realities of the USSR – its black past and its present incompetence. The media became more open, people were allowed greater freedom of speech and censored books were more available to the public. Political dissidents were recalled from exile. In 1986 the physicist and dissident Andrey Sakharov was allowed to return to Moscow from internal exile. Most challenging of all, Stalin's numerous crimes came to light. Records of repressions and corruption were revealed. Bukharin was posthumously rehabilitated and found innocent of the charges Stalin brought against him. However, the political openness championed by Gorbachev soon allowed critics to voice their opposition to Gorbachev's policies in public.

Another part of Gorbachev's political reforms entailed the democratization of the political process. In 1989, Gorbachev established the Congress of People's Deputies as the Soviet Union's highest legislative body. Gorbachev intended to introduce political representation to the Soviet political system. The new Congress had 2,250 deputies, 750 representing districts based on equal population, 750 representing districts based ethnic subdivisions and the newly-included 750 representing public organizations like the trade unions and the Academy of Sciences. While this body would be too large to sit permanently, the Congress would elect a 542-member Supreme Soviet which would serve as the permanent legislature, sitting for eight months a year. Elections to the Congress were held in March 1989 and marked a return of multi-party politics in Russia for the first time since the revolution. When the Congress opened on 25 May, it became the scene for passionate political debates. Members of the democratic opposition criticized Gorbachev for being too cautious in his reforms and called for the dissolution of the Communist Party. The democratic opposition's most prominent leaders were Andrey Sakharov, who had been elected to represent the Academy of Sciences, and Boris Yeltsin, a former ally of Gorbachev who was elected with 90% of the vote in his Moscow constituency.

When Sakharov died at the end of 1989, Yeltsin became the sole leader of the democratic opposition to Gorbachev. The same age as Gorbachev, Yeltsin had joined the Communist Party in 1961 and was the party chief of Sverdlovsk (Ekaterinburg) from 1976 to 1985. He was then summoned by Gorbachev to become Moscow party chief and a non-voting member of the Politburo. During this time, he was an outspoken campaigner against corruption in the party and clashed with Yegor Ligachev, who believed that glasnost had undermined the party system and risked the collapse of the Soviet Union itself. In October 1987 Yeltsin launched a bitter attack against Gorbachev at the Central Committee for failing to press ahead with the reforms. The incident led to Yeltsin's dismissal as Moscow party boss and his departure from the Politburo the following year. At the 19th party conference in 1988, Ligachev addressed Yeltsin and declared "Boris, you are wrong," which subsequently became a popular political catchphrase. Yeltsin's election to the Congress in

1989 marked his return from the political wilderness. He was subsequently elected to leading positions in the Russian Soviet Federative Socialist Republic (RSFSR), establishing an institutional power base to challenge Gorbachev. At the 28th Party Congress in July 1990, he made a dramatic speech to resign from the Communist Party and called for Gorbachev's resignation in the process.

Gorbachev met with opposition from the right as well as the left. His economic reforms resulted in the increase in prices of basic necessities. The workers soon called for higher wages to pay for goods, leading to inevitable inflation. Meanwhile, as a result of glasnost, the Soviet people had greater access to the western world and saw the contrast between their lives and the lives of those in the western world. The public started to lose their trust in the government. These developments caused anxiety among Communist Party officials who believed that Gorbachev was undermining the state. In 1990 Gorbachev created the office of President of the Soviet Union to reduce his dependence on party mechanisms. In response to secessionist pressures in the Baltic, Gorbachev also brokered a new union treaty which allowed the soviet republics greater levels of national autonomy. This was the final straw for the hardliners who staged a coup in August 1991 on the eve of signing ceremony of the new union treaty. Gorbachev was on holiday in Crimea when he was met by members of Politburo and the heads of the military and security services who placed him under house arrest. The coup leaders announced to the media that Gorbachev could no longer assume his position due to ill health, and established the Committee of the State of Emergency under Vice President Gennady Yanayev to assume control of the government. Gorbachev could do no more than to follow events by listening to the radio broadcast by the BBC World Service. Meanwhile, Yeltsin rushed to the Russian White House, which was home to the Congress of People's Deputies. When the plotters sent tanks against the parliament, Yeltsin defiantly climbed onto a tank and talked to the soldiers, many of whom abandoned their vehicles and joined the resistance to the coup. The coup failed and Gorbachev returned to Moscow, but Yeltsin had established himself as the most powerful political figure in the country.

Before the August coup, the Soviet Union and the Communist Party continued to enjoy some degree of public support. Following the coup, the Communist Party was disbanded and outlawed, while secessionist pressures increased. These pressures were strongest in the Baltic nations of Estonia, Latvia and Lithuania, which began to claim their right to freely secede from the USSR in 1990, having been forcibly incorporated into the Soviet Union during the Second World War under the terms of the Nazi-Soviet Pact. The first demonstrations were as early as 1986, starting from Riga and soon Tallinn. The Supreme Soviets of each Baltic States made their own language the state language again in early 1989 and the republics aimed for sovereignty. In August 1989 approximately two million people linked hands to form a human chain known as the Baltic Way between Vilnius and Tallinn, singing folk songs as a means of expressing their national identity. In March 1990, Lithuania was the first to declare independence, followed by Estonia at the end of the month and Latvia in May. Gorbachev attempted negotiations, but the Russian federal republic under Yeltsin proclaimed its own sovereignty in June 1990. The negotiations would change hands and fall to the new Russian republic. This threatened the Soviets and caused them to send the military in Baltic States in January 1991, resulting in the Vilnius Massacre in Lithuania and the Barricades in Latvia, in which hundreds of civilians were injured. It was only after the failed coup of August 1991 that the Baltic States were recognized as independent states.

The failed coup resulted in an exodus of national republics from the Soviet Union, as Moldavia, Georgia and Armenia also proclaimed their sovereignty. Gorbachev attempted to negotiate a new union treaty which aimed to establish a Union of Sovereign States. Once again, Gorbachev's attempts to preserve a form of union were hijacked, this time by Yeltsin. On 7 December Yeltsin met the presidents of Ukraine and Belarus in the Belorussian state dacha near

Belovezh. The following day they signed the Belovezh Accords, which declared the dissolution of the USSR and the creation of Commonwealth of Independent States (CIS), a far looser association than Gorbachev had intended. Yeltsin fatally weakened Gorbachev's authority and the latter lacked the power to resist. The Russian government soon assumed all functions of the Soviet government with the exception of defense and nuclear energy, as ordered by Yeltsin on 19 December. On 21 December, 11 of 12 remaining republics (with the exception of Georgia) would sign the foundation documents of the CIS in Almaty, Kazakhstan. Gorbachev resigned the office of President of the Soviet Union on 25 December 1991. Less than an hour later, the hammer-and-sickle flag was lowered, this time forever, and replaced with the tricolor of Russia. USSR's seat in the UN Security Council was succeeded by Russia. Soviet embassies were changed into Russian embassies. The Soviet Union was formally dissolved on 31 December 1991.

The collapse of the Soviet Union came as a surprise to western observers. Although Gorbachev's political popularity plummeted during 1991, he remained highly respected among political leaders in the west. During his rule over the Soviet Union, Gorbachev's foreign policy was aimed at establishing closer relationships with western countries. The de-escalation of the Cold War would allow him to divert funds away from the armed forces towards his domestic reform program. In 1988 he announced the withdrawal of Soviet forces from Afghanistan, with Soviet involvement ending the following year. Moreover, Gorbachev actively sought out advice about free markets from western economists. For their part, western political leaders appreciated that Gorbachev was a man whom, in the words of UK Prime Minister Margaret Thatcher, they could "do business with." In October 1986 Gorbachev met with US President Ronald Reagan to discuss arms reduction at a summit in Reykjavik which led to a commitment to eliminate nuclear weapons within ten years. Gorbachev's most consequential foreign policy decision was to abandon the Soviet policy of intervention in Eastern Europe. As a result, over the course of 1989 a number of Eastern European countries, beginning with Poland, overthrew their Communist governments without Soviet interference. The Berlin Wall was dismantled in 1989 and the two Germanies agreed to unification in 1990. The collapse of communism in Eastern Europe and the dissolution of the Soviet Union in 1991 marked the end of the Cold War. Western observers gave Gorbachev credit for managing the transition to democracy largely without bloodshed, with the exception of the attempt to suppress the revolutions in the Baltic. With the collapse of communism, Russians and Americans alike anticipated a new era of peace and prosperity based on liberal democracy and free-market capitalism.

Conclusion

Following the collapse of the Soviet Union in 1992, a feeling of hope swept through the newly instituted Russian Federation. However, this feeling soon turned sour. Yeltsin's reforms to the Russian economy led to hyperinflation and rendered savings and pensions worthless. Yeltsin soon encountered opposition to his policies from the Russian Congress of People's Deputies, resulting in a constitutional crisis. In 1993 Yeltsin sent tanks against the parliament, which had voted to impeach him for acting unconstitutionally. The sight of Yeltsin attacking the very building which he so defiantly defended two years earlier was a bitter pill to swallow for many Russian democrats. By the presidential election in 1996, Yeltsin seemed likely to lose to his main rival, Gennady Zyuganov, leader of the Russian Communist Party. In order to stave off defeat, he made a deal with the oligarchs, a class of businessmen and former bureaucrats who profited from the privatization of state industries at the expense of the Russian people. Although Yeltsin won the election, he continued to be unpopular while the economy remained volatile. In August 1998 the Russian government had no choice but to default on its debt. For many Russians who were now destitute with minimal state support, the capitalist experiment seemed like a failure. On 31 December 1999, Yeltsin suddenly resigned from the presidency four months before the end of his term and appointed his Prime Minister Vladimir Putin as his acting successor. Putin won the subsequent election convincingly to become President of Russia.

Vladimir Putin was a relatively unknown entity when Yeltsin appointed him Prime Minister in August 1999. A former KGB officer who served in East Germany, Putin was an advisor to the liberal Mayor of St. Petersburg Anatoly Sobchak following the Soviet collapse. During the early years of his presidency, Putin seemed to continue down the path of economic reform. Putin's presidency has been characterized by centralization of power. He launched a campaign against the oligarchs by claiming that they were stealing from the Russian people. The most high-profile conflict was against Mikhail Khordokovsky, the chief of the Yukos oil company and the richest man in Russia. Khordokovsky was arrested in 2003 on corruption charges and the assets of his oil business were transferred to the state-owned company Rosneft, chaired by Igor Sechin, a former KGB officer and one of Putin's closest advisors. Putin's war against the oligarchs was popular, although Putin supported the business interests of several oligarchs who were his political supporters, including Roman Abramovich, an energy magnate who bought Chelsea Football Club in 2003. Putin's actions courted controversy, but he presided over an economic boom. Rising oil prices boosted the Russian economy and Putin enjoyed approval ratings of over 70 percent. When he was forced by constitutional requirements to stand down from the presidency in 2008, he supported the candidacy of Dmitry Medvedev and became Prime Minister. He returned to the presidency in 2012 amid protests that he was seeking to become a dictator. Medvedev presided over a constitutional change which extended presidential terms to six years. As a result, Putin could serve as President until 2024.

Putin continues to court controversy and suspicion in the western world, especially after the occupation of Crimea in 2014. Alleged Russian state involvement in the 2016 US presidential elections has also led to a sense of unease, which was amplified following the attempted assassination of former Russian intelligence officer Sergey Skripal in England in 2018. Putin's centralization of power has caused many political commentators and historians to argue that Russia has an autocratic political tradition and is by nature suspicious of democracy. A closer examination of eleven centuries of Russian history leads to a more nuanced conclusion. Modern Russia, as a continental entity centered in Moscow, only began to develop in the 15th and 16th centuries. The attempts by grand princes, later tsars and emperors, to establish autocratic rule, were resisted fiercely by fellow princes and nobles. In order to get their way, sovereigns would appeal to the people in their capacity as divinely-appointed rulers. Such efforts were also reflected in Lenin and Stalin's appeals to the people over the party elites, and Putin's efforts to strip away the power of the oligarchs in the name of the people. Nevertheless, these attempts at autocratic government had their limits. Voltaire famously remarked that the Russian government was "autocracy tempered by assassination." Russian rulers throughout the centuries, however formidable they seemed, had to broker informal power-sharing settlements with magnates if they were to avoid palace coups. The tension between autocratic and oligarchic tendencies is a key theme that runs throughout Russian history but is by no means unique to Russia.

Another key thread of Russian history is the tension between Orthodoxy and pluralism. Russia is often seen as a conservative society resistant to changes in social values. Certainly, ever since the times of Prince Vladimir, Orthodox Christianity was a defining feature of Russian identity. The influence of the Church in local education continued until the beginning of the twentieth century.

Despite this, Russia has always been a multicultural and multiethnic state. The Russian Empire's expansion to the south resulted in the incorporation of large Muslim populations, while westward expansion resulted in an influx of Catholic believers. Jews and Buddhists have also lived in Russia for many centuries. Despite its reputation for conservatism, Russia has produced some of the world's most radical thinkers and innovators. These individuals included monarchs such as Peter the Great, but also revolutionaries in the form of Lenin and Trotsky. While the Soviet state exploited the religiosity of the Russian people to transform them into communist believers, it encouraged the study of sciences and the accumulation of secular knowledge.

Over the course of the past millennium, the Russian state has transformed from a collection of principalities centered in Kiev to a continental behemoth which straddles Europe and Asia. Russia's status as a geographical anomaly which is neither entirely European nor fully Asian has prompted efforts to create a uniquely Russian sense of identity. A quarter of a century after the collapse of the Soviet Union, Russia finds itself at a crossroads. In order to establish political legitimacy, Putin has borrowed the symbols of medieval, imperial, and Soviet Russia. In 2016 he unveiled a giant statue of Prince Vladimir the Great outside the Kremlin. He has sanctioned the cult of Nicholas II and has provided the Russian Orthodox Church with a prominent role in social life. At the same time, he continues to pay tribute to the Soviet legacy and considers the victory against Nazi Germany as one of the great legacies of the Soviet state. In Moscow's Red Square the skyline is shared by imperial eagles and communist red stars. Although Putin appears to have established a stable government based on conservatism and nationalism, the tensions that have determined the course of Russian history continue under the surface. It is difficult for anyone to predict the course of Russia's future, but it is likely to be as dramatic as its past.

Here's another book by Captivating History that we think you'd be interested in

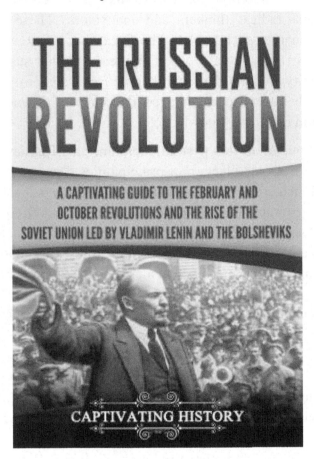

Further Reading

General Russian History

Figes, O., *Natasha's Dance: A Cultural History of Russia* (New York, 2003).

Freeze, G., *Russia: A History* (Oxford, 2009).

Riasanovsky, N., *A History of Russia* (New York, 1977).

Part 1 – Medieval Rus

Fennell, J.L.I, *The emergence of Moscow 1304-1359* (Los Angeles, 1968).

Franklin, F. & Shephard, J. *The Emergence of Rus, 750-1200* (New York, 1996).

Halperin, C.J., *Russia and the Golden Horde: The Mongol Impact on Medieval Russian History* (Bloomington, 1985).

Martin, J., *Medieval Russia, 980-1584, Second Edition* (Cambridge, 2007).

Vernadsky, G.A., *Kievan Russia* (New Haven, 1948).

Part 2 – Romanov Russia

Dixon, S., *Catherine the Great* (London, 2009).

Figes, O., *A People's Tragedy: The Russian Revolution 1891-1924* (London, 1997).

Lieven, D.C.B., *Russia Against Napoleon* (London, 2009).

Lieven, D.C.B., *Towards the Flame: Empire, War and the End of Tsarist Russia* (London, 2016).

Massie, R.K., *Peter the Great* (New York, 1981).

Platonov, S.F., *The Time of Troubles: Historical Study of the Internal Crisis and Social Struggles in Sixteenth and Seventeenth Century Muscovy* (Lawrence, 1970).

Radzinsky, E.S., *Alexander II: The Last Great Tsar* (New York, 2006).

Sebag Montefiore, S., *The Romanovs* (London, 2016).

Part 3 – Soviet Russia

Brown, A., *The Rise and Fall of Communism* (New York, 2009).

Brown, A., *The Gorbachev Factor* (Oxford, 1996).

Sebag Montefiore, S., *Stalin: Court of the Red Tsar* (London, 2005).

Service, R., *Lenin: A Biography* (London, 2000).

Service, R., *The Penguin History of Modern Russia: From Tsarism to the Twenty-First Century, Third Edition* (London, 2009).

Free Bonus from Captivating History (Available for a Limited time)

Hi History Lovers!

Now you have a chance to join our exclusive history list so you can get your first history ebook for free as well as discounts and a potential to get more history books for free! Simply visit the link below to join.

Captivatinghistory.com/ebook

Also, make sure to follow us on:

Twitter: @Captivhistory

Facebook: Captivating History:@captivatinghistory

Made in the USA
Las Vegas, NV
31 March 2022

46633128R00085